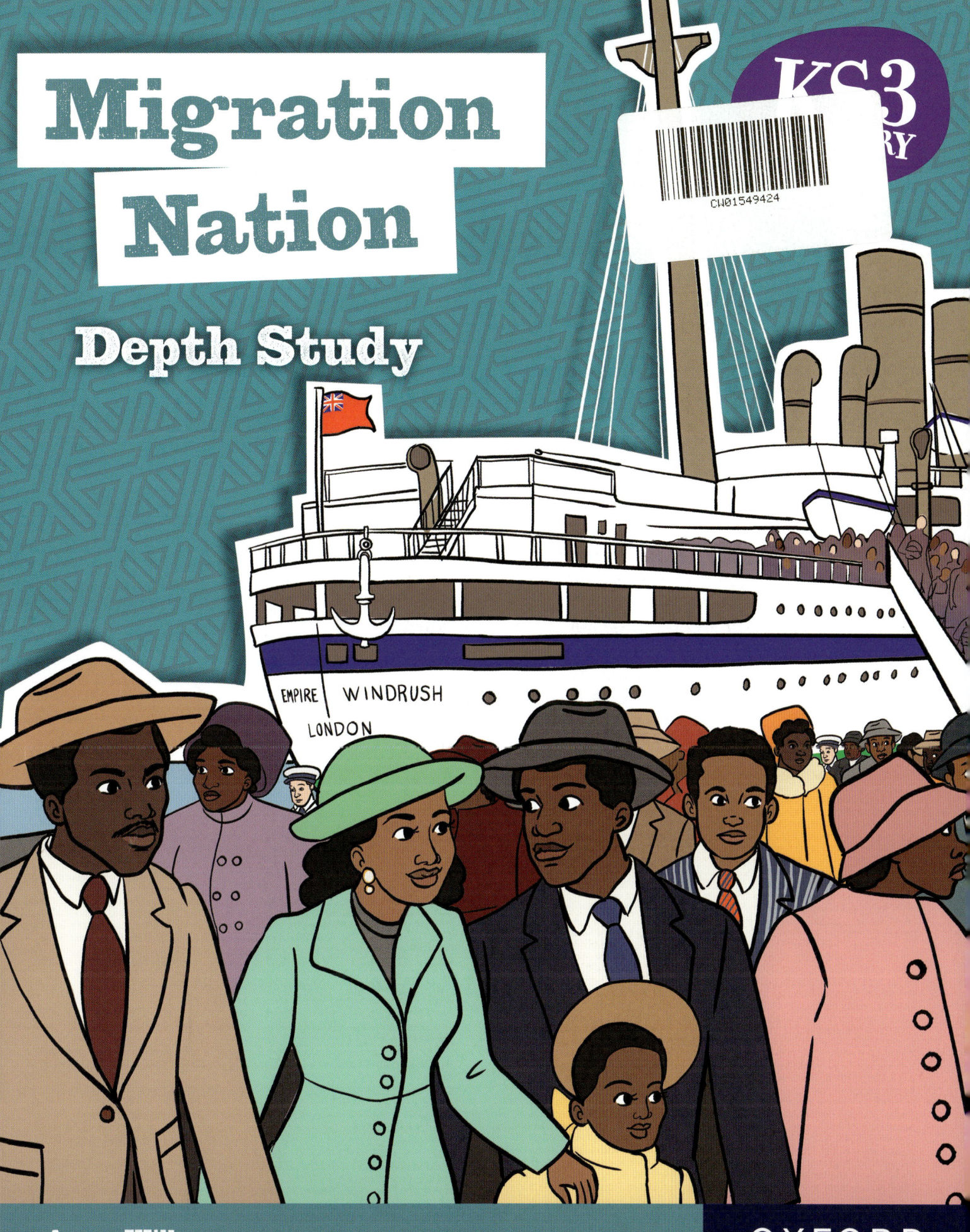

OXFORD
UNIVERSITY PRESS

Great Clarendon Street, Oxford, OX2 6DP, United Kingdom

Oxford University Press is a department of the University of Oxford. It furthers the University's objective of excellence in research, scholarship, and education by publishing worldwide. Oxford is a registered trade mark of Oxford University Press in the UK and in certain other countries.

© Oxford University Press 2023

The moral rights of the author have been asserted

First published in 2023

All rights reserved. No part of this publication may be reproduced, stored in a retrieval system, or transmitted, in any form or by any means, without the prior permission in writing of Oxford University Press, or as expressly permitted by law, by licence or under terms agreed with the appropriate reprographics rights organization. Enquiries concerning reproduction outside the scope of the above should be sent to the Rights Department, Oxford University Press, at the address above.

You must not circulate this work in any other form and you must impose this same condition on any acquirer

British Library Cataloguing in Publication Data
Data available

978-1-382-04242-0

978-1-382-04240-6 (ebook)

978-1-382-04241-3 (Kerboodle digital book)

10 9 8 7 6 5 4 3 2 1

MIX
Paper | Supporting responsible forestry
FSC www.fsc.org FSC® C007785

The manufacturing process conforms to the environmental regulations of the country of origin.

Printed in the United Kingdom by Bell & Bain

Acknowledgements

The publisher would like to thank the following for permissions to use copyright material:

Audrey Gillan: Extract from 'Day the East End said 'No pasaran' to Blackshirts', by Audrey Gillan, published by The Guardian, 30 September 2006. Copyright Guardian News & Media Ltd 2023. Reproduced by permission of Guardian News & Media Ltd. **Matthew Calfe:** Extract from 'The Navvies: How the Irish built the modern British railways' by Matthew Calfe, published by IrishCentral, 7 September 2015. Reproduced by permission of the publisher. **The Guardian:** Extract from 'West Indians arrive in Britain on board the Empire Windrush' – archive, 1948, published by The Guardian, 23 June 2016. Copyright Guardian News & Media Ltd 2023. Reproduced by permission of Guardian News & Media Ltd. **Linda McDowell:** Extract from 'How Caribbean migrants helped to rebuild Britain', by Linda McDowell, published by British Library, 4 October 2018. Reproduced by permission of the British Library. **Sam King:** Extract from Interview with WWII Veteran Sam King, interviewed by the BBC in 1998. Reproduced by permission of BBC. **Sarfraz Manzoor:** Extract from 'Black Britain's darkest hour' by Sarfraz Manzoor, published by The Guardian, 24 February 2008. Copyright Guardian News & Media Ltd 2023. Reproduced by permission of Guardian News & Media Ltd. **Amelia Gentleman:** Extract from "They erased a bit of my life': Windrush generation on Home Office treatment' by Amelia Gentleman, published by The Guardian, 18 July 2018. Copyright Guardian News & Media Ltd 2023. Reproduced by permission of Guardian News & Media Ltd. **International Rescue Committee:** Extract from a video transcription from 'Refugee Conversations: Ukrainian mother and son discuss fleeing the war and life in the UK', published on rescue.org. Reproduced by permission of International Rescue Committee, Inc. Anti-Slavery International: Extract from 'What is Modern Slavery?', published on antislavery.org. Reproduced by permission of Anti-Slavery International. **Dr Onyeka Nubia:** Extract from 'Who were the African people living in Medieval and Tudor England?', by Dr Onyeka Nubia, published by BBC. Reproduced by permission of Dr Onyeka Nubia. **Miranda Kaufman:** Extract from 'Black Tudors: The Untold Story' by historian Miranda Kaufman, published by Oneworld Publications. Reproduced by permission of the publisher. **Sasha Mistlin:** Extract from 'We're still dealing with perceptions of what Black can be' by Sasha Mistlin, published by The Guardian, 5 November 2021. Copyright Guardian News & Media Ltd 2023. Reproduced by permission of Guardian News & Media Ltd. **BBC News:** Extract from 'Immigration 'harming communities'', published by BBC News. Reproduced by permission of BBC News at bbc.co.uk/news. **Bart Édes:** Extract from 'Migrant Workers: Doing the Dirty Work for Others' by Bart Édes, published by Asian Development Blog. Reproduced by permission of Asian Development Bank. **Susheila Nasta**, **Dr Florian Stadtler** and **Rozina Visram:** Extract from 'Culture and intellectual life', by Susheila Nasta, Dr Florian Stadtler, Rozina Visram, published by British Library, July 2017. Reproduced by permission of British Library. **Gilli Salvat:** Extract from audio transcript of 'Immigration from India 1948: Gilli Salvat talks about travelling from India to England in 1948', published by British Library. Reproduced by permission of British Library. **Abdul Aslam:** Extract from 'Migration From Kashmir to Pakistan and then to Bradford, 1950-1969' by Abdul Aslam, The National Archives (archived 5 November 2013). Reproduced under Open Government Licence. **The National Archives:** Extract from 'People Today Wear Their Pyjamas on the Road, 1957-2006' by Mr Laxman, The National Archives (archived 6 November 2013). Reproduced under Open Government Licence. **BBC archives:** Extract from 'Immigration and Emigration: Journey to Leicester', BBC archives, 18 June 2014. Reproduced by permission of BBC. **Jeevan Panesar:** Extract from 'A History of Leicester' by Jeevan Panesar, BBC Online, 2 November 2005. Reproduced by permission of BBC. **Nik Kotecha:** Extract from '"Back home" is Uganda to me, 1950-2006' by Nik Kotecha, The National Archives (archived 6 November 2013). Reproduced under Open Government Licence. **Ben Riley-Smith:** Extract from 'Eastern European immigrants 'overwhelming benefit UK economy" By Ben Riley-Smith, published by The Telegraph, 29 November 2013. © The Telegraph Media Group Limited 2023. Reproduced by permission of the publisher. **K Muirhead:** Quote by K. Muirhead, 2021. Reproduced with permission from K. Muirhead. **George Parker**, **Robert Wright**, **James Shotter**, **Andy Bounds**, **Judith Evans** and **Alice Hancock:** Extract from 'How two decades of EU migration went into reverse' by George Parker, Robert Wright, James Shotter, Andy Bounds, Judith Evans and Alice Hancock, published by Financial Times. © The Financial Times Ltd 2023. Reproduced by permission of the publisher.

Cover illustrations: Chanté Timothy / Darley Anderson Illustration Agency

Photos: p6(t): Heritage Image Partnership Ltd / Alamy Stock Photo; **p6(b):** IanDagnall Computing / Alamy Stock Photo; **p7(l):** Chronicle / Alamy Stock Photo; **7(r):** Keystone Press / Alamy Stock Photo; **p8:** PA Images / Alamy Stock Photo; **p11:** Contains public sector information licensed under the Open Government Licence v1.0.; **p13(Source B):** Chronicle / Alamy Stock Photo; **p13(Source C):** PBL Collection / Alamy Stock Photo; **p15(Source B):** David Lichtneker / Alamy Stock Photo; **p15(Source C):** GRANGER - Historical Picture Archive / Alamy Stock Photo; **p18:** travellinglight / Alamy Stock Photo; **p19:** World History Archive / Alamy Stock Photo; **p20:** Heritage Image Partnership Ltd / Alamy Stock Photo; **p21:** Handout / Getty; **p22:** RBM Vintage Images / Alamy Stock Photo; **p23:** David Savill / Stringer / Getty; **p24(Source A):** Eden Breitz / Alamy Stock Photo; **p24(Source C):** Heritage Image Partnership Ltd / Alamy Stock Photo; **p25(Source D):** GRANGER - Historical Picture Archive / Alamy Stock Photo; **p25(Source E):** Matthew Horwood / Alamy Stock Photo; **p25(Source F):** PA Images / Alamy Stock Photo; **p25(Source H):** PA Images / Alamy Stock Photo; **p26:** travellinglight / Alamy Stock Photo; **p27:** Jewish Museum London; **p28(Source A):** Maidun Collection / Alamy Stock Photo; **p28(Source B):** Mick Sinclair / Alamy Stock Photo; **p29(Source C):** Chronicle / Alamy Stock Photo; **p29(Source D):** Trinity Mirror / Mirrorpix / Alamy Stock Photo; **p30(S ource E):** Ian Goodrick / Alamy Stock Photo; **p30(Source F):** A.P.S. (UK) / Alamy Stock Photo; **30(Source G):** Paul Popper / Popperfoto / Contributor / Getty Images; **p31(Source H):** PA Images / Alamy Stock Photo; **p31(Source I):** Tim E White / Alamy Stock Photo; **p31**(Source J): Associated Press / Alamy Stock Photo; **p33(Source A):** De Luan / Alamy Stock Photo; **p33(Source B):** Ira Berger / Alamy Stock Photo; **p34:** British Railways - S. W. A. Newton Collection; **p35:** PA Images / Alamy Stock Photo; **p37(Source B):** PictureLux / The Hollywood Archive / Alamy Stock Photo; **p37(Source C):** Simon Hadley / Alamy Stock Photo; **p37(Source D):** London Entertainment / Alamy Stock Photo; **p38:** British Railways - S. W. A. Newton Collection; **p40(Source A):** GRANGER - Historical Picture Archive / Alamy Stock Photo; **p40(Interpretation B):** Aaron Watson & University of Reading; **p42:** College of Arms MS Westminster Tournament Roll, 1511. Reproduced by permission of the Kings, Heralds and Pursuivants of Arms; **p43:** agefotostock / Alamy Stock Photo; **p45(Source B):** PjrStatues / Alamy Stock Photo; **p45(Source C):** Popperfoto / Contributor / Getty; **p46:** World History Archive / Alamy Stock Photo; **p48:** London Metropolitan University Library Services and Special Collections; **p49:** ANL/Shutterstock; **p50:** Crown Copyright / Courtesy of the BFI National Archive; **p51:** Steve Taylor ARPS / Alamy Stock Photo; **p52:** PA Images / Alamy Stock Photo; **p53:** David Thickins; **p54:** James Boardman Archive / Alamy Stock Photo; **p55:** Keystone Press / Alamy Stock Photo; **p55(Source B):** Alex Cavendish / Alamy Stock Photo; **p56(Source A):** FPG/Staff/Getty Images; **p56(Source B):** OnTheRoad / Alamy Stock Photo; **p57(Source D):** PA Images / Alamy Stock Photo; **p57(Source E):** PA Images / Alamy Stock Photo; **p57(Source F):** PA Images / Alamy Stock Photo; **p57(Source G):** Goldsmiths, University of London; **p57(Source H):** PA Images / Alamy Stock Photo; **p57(Source I):** Steven May / Alamy Stock Photo; **p58:** Alex Cavendish / Alamy Stock Photo; **p63(Source B):** Photo 12 / Alamy Stock Photo; **p63(Source C):** incamerastock / Alamy Stock Photo; **p64:** Moviestore / Shutterstock; **p65(Source E):** BFA / Alamy Stock Photo; **p65(Source F, a):** Daily Express / Reach Licensing; **p65(Source F, b):** Daily Express / Reach Licensing ; **p66(Source A):** Atomic / Alamy Stock Photo; **p66(Source B):** Paul Popper /Popperfoto / Contributor / Getty Images; **p67(Source C):** Pictorial Press Ltd / Alamy Stock Photo; **p67(Source D):** Dinodia Photos / Alamy Stock Photo; **p67(Source E):** The Picture Art Collection / Alamy Stock Photo; **p67(Source F):** Eraza Collection / Alamy Stock Photo; **p67(Source G):** Historic Images / Alamy Stock Photo; **p68:** Evening Standard / Stringer / Getty Images; **p69:** Popperfoto / Contributor / Getty Images; **p71:** Source: People's History Musuem / Copyright unknown; **p72:** GRANGER - Historical Picture Archive / Alamy Stock Photo; **p73:** Keystone Press / Alamy Stock Photo; **p74(Source A):** Allan Cash Picture Library / Alamy Stock Photo; **p74 (Source C):** Guy Bell / Alamy Stock Photo; **p75:** Suzie Gibbons / Contributor / Getty Images; **p76:** Popperfoto / Contributor / Getty Images; **p81(Source A):** Attribution-NonCommercial-ShareAlike 4.0 International (CC BY-NC-SA 4.0); **p81(Source B):** incamerastock / Alamy Stock Photo; **p81(Source C):** CBW / Alamy Stock Photo; **p81(Source D):** Ian Nellist / Alamy Stock Photo; **p82:** Source: Polish Resettlement Camps in the UK / Copyright Unknown; **p83(Source F):** Source: Polish Resettlement Camps in the UK / Copyright Unknown; **p83(Source H):** David Bagnall / Alamy Stock Photo; **p87:** clynt Garnham Agriculture / Alamy Stock Photo; **p88:** David Bagnall / Alamy Stock Photo; **p93:** Independent / Alamy Stock Photo.

Artwork by Rudolf Farkas, Kamae Design, and Q2A Media.

Every effort has been made to contact copyright holders of material reproduced in this book. Any omissions will be rectified in subsequent printings if notice is given to the publisher.

Links to third party websites are provided by Oxford in good faith and for information only. Oxford disclaims any responsibility for the materials contained in any third party website referenced in this work.

From the author: Aaron would like the thank the brilliant Polly Coupar-Hennessy, Emma Jones and Alison Schrecker at Oxford University Press for all their fantastic ideas, hard work and excellent suggestions at every stage of this project. In addition, I would also like to thank Steve Day, one of my own history teachers. It was Steve (or Mr. Day) who opened my eyes to this wonderful subject, and whose enthusiasm and passion for the subject inspired me more than he could imagine.

The publisher would like to thank the following people for offering their contribution into the development of this book: the Learning Team from the Migration Museum, Arthur Torrington CBE, Melanie Waldron, David Rawlings and James Helling.

The publisher would also like to thank the following people for their careful review of relevant sections of this book: Tony Kushner, Miri Rubin, Meleisa Ono-George, Sumita Mukherjee, Kathy Burrell, Jack Hepworth and Emily Manktelow. We are very grateful for their careful reviews and valuable input.

Contents

Introduction 4
Timeline 6

Big Question 1: What is migration? 8
Big Question 2: Why should we study migration? 12
Big Question 3: Who were the earliest migrants to Britain? 14

Chapter 1: Jewish migration
1.1 The first Jewish community in England 18
1.2 The return of Jewish people 20
1.3 The Battle of Cable Street 22
1.4 Jewish people in modern Britain 24
1 Have you been learning? 26
Big Question 4: Why have migrants come to Britain? 28

Chapter 2: Irish migration
2.1 The Great Hunger 32
2.2 How did Irish people help build Britain? 34
2.3 Irish people in modern Britain 36
2 Have you been learning? 38
Big Question 5: Why did Black people migrate to Britain before the twentieth century? 40

Chapter 3: Caribbean migration
3.1 Caribbean migration before the Second World War 44
3.2A/B The Windrush generation 46
3.3A/B The Caribbean experience in the 1950s, 1960s and 1970s 50
3.4 The fight against prejudice 54
3.5 Activism and achievement 56
3 Have you been learning? 58
Big Question 6: How has migration changed Britain? 60
Big Question 7: How has migration been portrayed in the media? 62

Chapter 4: South Asian migration
4.1 Britain and South Asia 66
4.2A/B The South Asian experience 68
4.3 South Asian people in East Africa 72
4.4 South Asian people in Britain today 74
4 Have you been learning? 76
Big Question 8: Which migrant groups have arrived in Britain in recent years? 78

Chapter 5: Eastern European migration
5.1A/B Eastern European migration to Britain before and after the Second World War 80
5.2 The EU and Eastern European migration 84
5.3 Eastern Europeans in Britain today 86
5 Have you been learning? 88
Big Question 9: Why is migration a controversial topic? 90

Glossary 94
Index 95

Introducing KS3 History Depth Studies: Migration Nation

What is this book about?

This textbook tells the story of a number of different groups of people who have migrated (moved) to the United Kingdom. It covers a huge period of time – from the migration of Jewish people from Europe in the twelfth century to migration from Eastern Europe in the twenty-first century. That's almost a thousand years of history!

This textbook focuses mainly on the following groups of people who migrated to the UK: Jewish people; Irish people; people from the Caribbean; people from South Asia; people from Eastern Europe. Of course, these are not the only people who have migrated to the UK. For centuries, people have migrated to the UK from all over the world. We couldn't fit all of this into one textbook, but we hope that looking at some of these stories will help you learn about migration more generally.

We are also conscious that migrants and their descendants have multilayered identities and that the ways we have chosen to describe them may not be the way they choose to describe themselves. Nevertheless, all those living in Britain today are descended from people who migrated to this country, and we hope you see echoes of your family's migration story in this textbook.

Using this book

This book will get you thinking. Some of the things you look at will challenge you. Some things might really surprise (or even shock) you – or get you thinking in a different way. You will be asked to look at different pieces of evidence and to try to work things out for yourself. Sometimes, two pieces of evidence about the same event won't agree with each other. You might be asked to think of reasons why that is. Your answers might not be the same as your friend's or even your teacher's. This is okay. The important thing is to give reasons for your thoughts and ideas.

Getting the history right

We have consulted lots of experts to ensure that the content of this book is as accurate as possible and reflects the latest 'historical scholarship' (historians writing about history). Historians who have helped us include Tony Kushner (University of Southampton), Miri Rubin (Queen Mary, University of London), Meleisa Ono-George (University of Oxford), Sumita Mukherjee (University of Bristol), Kathy Burrell (University of Liverpool), Jack Hepworth (University of Oxford) and Emily Manktelow (Royal Holloway, University of London). We have also worked with Arthur Torrington CBE (co-founder of the Windrush Foundation) and the Learning Team at the Migration Museum.

There's another thing that's important to mention when we study migration – the story isn't fixed. It is constantly developing as historians think more deeply about migration and uncover rich stories about the people who were – and are – part of the migration story. History has always been told from a variety of perspectives and new interpretations and views are always being added to our collective migration story. I hope we've managed to show you a thorough picture. We've tried to ensure that the voices of people who migrated to Britain are at the heart of this book so they can share their experiences and explain how their migration story has had an impact on their lives.

Aaron Wilkes

Key features

Earlier on... / Meanwhile... / Later on... 1700
You will be challenged to think how the topic you are studying relates to events, people, ideas or developments that may have happened many years before, at the same time, or years later.

Key Words These are important words and terms that are vital to help you understand the topics. You can spot them easily because they are in bold red type. Look up their meanings in the glossary at the back of the book.

Objectives All lessons in this book start by setting you objectives. These are your key aims that set out your learning targets for the work ahead.

Over to You These activities are an opportunity for you to demonstrate your knowledge and understanding of the history you've been learning. In each box the tasks become progressively more challenging.

Fact ✓ These are fascinating little bits of history that you don't usually get to hear about! They give you extra insights into topics and challenge the way you think.

History Skills ★ These activities test a range of history skills, so each box has its own title. The tasks will challenge you to think a little deeper about what you have been studying. These are also important skills to develop if you are going to study GCSE History.

Big Question You will come across some 'Big Questions' about migration. These will make you think really hard about some of the big ideas, themes and questions related to migration.

Connections These give you an idea of what was happening in other parts of the world, at the same time as the period you are studying. It will help you draw parallels between the topic you are currently studying and other historical topics.

Have you been learning?

There are different types of assessments at the end of every chapter. These are opportunities for you to showcase what you have learned and to put your ability to recall key information and history skills to the test.

 Quick Knowledge Quiz These short tests will give you a quick snapshot of what you have remembered about the chapter.

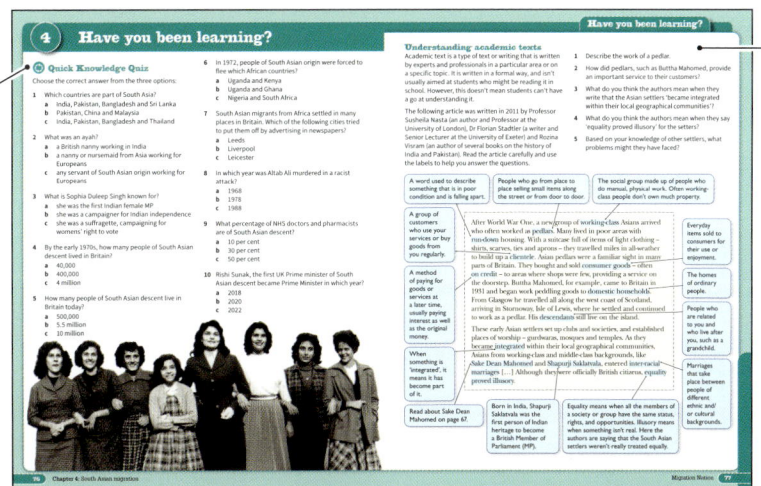

In-depth activities These activities will test your knowledge and understanding of the chapter in more depth. They will also help you develop key literacy skills such as making inferences and writing in detail.

Migration Nation

Timeline

It is thought that for hundreds of thousands of years, there were probably no humans in Britain at all. Then, about half a million years ago, people from Europe began to arrive. These were the earliest migrants to the British Isles. People with different cultures, beliefs and languages have continued to migrate to Britain since then. Therefore, anyone who lives in Britain today is descended from migrants who came from overseas to settle. So, the topic of migration is relevant to all of us because it is the history of all of us. Indeed, an understanding of the story of migration to Britain is essential to understanding the history of Britain and the country it is today.

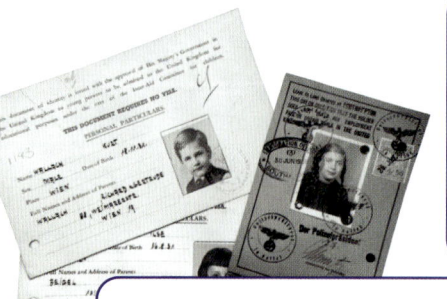

1947
The European Voluntary Workers (EVW) scheme is introduced. In total around 90,000 Eastern Europeans arrive in the first few years after the Second World War, mainly from Ukraine, Poland and Latvia.

1938–1939
The Kindertransport sees 10,000 children from Nazi-controlled territory arrive in Britain. Their parents are not allowed to come to Britain.

1905
Aliens Act is passed, which restricts immigration of 'undesirable immigrants'.

1840s
Large numbers of Irish migrants begin to arrive in Britain as a result of the Great Hunger (which is also known as the Irish Potato Famine).

43CE
The Romans, from Italy, invade Britain and soon conquer many of the existing tribes. They stay for around 400 years and much of Britain becomes part of the Roman Empire. Africans have been living in Britian since at least Roman times.

410CE
The Romans return to Italy. Britons see the arrival of new tribes from modern-day Denmark and northern Germany called Angles, Saxons and Jutes. Collectively, the invaders became known as Anglo-Saxons.

1655
Oliver Cromwell holds a conference and it is decided that Jews should be readmitted to England.

Before 43CE
Different migrant groups come to Britain for many thousands of years before the arrival of the Romans. Some come peacefully, while others are hostile. Some come for only a short time, but others settle for good. Those who settle on the British Isles are known as British people (or Britons).

865CE
Vikings (from what are now Denmark, Sweden and Norway) begin to invade and settle in Britain.

1965
Race Relations Act is passed – the first British law to directly address racism. It makes discrimination illegal on the grounds of 'colour, race or ethnic or national origins'.

1968
Commonwealth Immigrants Act is passed – Commonwealth immigrants are only allowed to live and work in Britain if they have a parent or grandparent who was born in Britain or was a British citizen.

1973
Britain joins the European Economic Community (EEC), which becomes the European Union (EU) in 1992.

2021
The UK leaves the European Union.

1972
Ugandan and Kenyan Asians begin to arrive in Britain after being expelled from their homes.

1948
Migrants from the Caribbean arrive in Britain on the *Empire Windrush*; British Nationality Act is passed, which makes all people living in Commonwealth countries British citizens.

1880s
Jews from Eastern Europe and Russia settle in the East End of London.

1572
French Protestants, called Huguenots, begin to settle in England.

1290
Edward I expels Jews from England.

1066
The Normans (from Normandy, a region of France) invade England and conquer the existing population. In 1070, Norman king, William the Conqueror, invites Jews from Normandy to settle in England.

Fact ✓

In this book, the word 'Britain' will generally be used instead of the term 'British Isles' when describing the nation as a whole. However, the largest island is now divided into different countries (England, Scotland and Wales), and the second largest island is made up of Northern Ireland (a part of the United Kingdom) and the Republic of Ireland (a separate, independent country).

Over to You

1 Working out which year is in which century can be tricky. The easiest way is to cover up the last two numbres in a year and add one to the first two numbers. For example, 1572 is in the sixteenth century (cover up the '72' and add one to 15 to make 16). Which century are the following years in?

   a 1066   c 1655   e 1905
   b 1290   d 1840

2 Which century were the following events in?
   a Jews from Eastern Europe and Russia settle in the East End.
   b The Romans return to Italy.
   c The UK leaves the European Union.
   d Migrants from the Caribbean arrive on the *Empire Windrush*.
   e The Vikings settle in Britain.

3 Now put the five events above into the correct chronological order.

Migration Nation

Big Question 1: What is migration?

Put simply, **migration** is the movement of people from one place to another – and a person who moves is known as a **migrant**. People have migrated for the whole of human history, whether that has been from one village to another, one region to another, from the countryside to the city, or across borders, seas and continents. During the course of human history, there has been a huge variety of reasons for migration: to live in an easier climate; to find better sources of food; to escape danger or hardship; to find work, or better work. Sometimes people have migrated alone, sometimes with a group. Some have moved because they wanted to, while others have moved because they had no choice and were forced to. Today, the United Nations estimates that 3.6 per cent of the world's population lives outside their country of birth. So, what are the different types of migration? What words are used to describe different types of migrants? And what do they mean?

Objectives
- Define 'voluntary migration' and 'forced migration'.
- Explore different ways people migrate from one country to another.

Voluntary or forced migration?

Generally speaking, we can put migration into two categories – 'forced' and 'voluntary'.

- Voluntary migration is when people choose to move. For example:
  - They might want to improve their chances of finding a job – or a better-paid job (these people are sometimes called economic migrants).
  - They might want to improve their quality of life – by living or working in a better environment or by moving to a country where there are better services such as healthcare or transport.
  - They may be encouraged to move by the government of another country – perhaps they are skilled tradespeople who are invited to set up a business in a different country, or they are filling job vacancies in vital industries.
- Forced migration is when people have little or no choice but to move. For example:
  - They may have to leave their homeland because of natural disasters such as floods or earthquakes.
  - They might belong to a group, race or religion that is facing **persecution** in their own country and are afraid that they will be harmed or killed if they stay there.
  - They may be fleeing from dangers such as war or famine.
  - They may be brought to a country against their will – as an enslaved person, for example.

Fact ✓
According to the United Nations, four out of five refugees stay close to their country of origin. In 2023, Türkiye (Turkey) hosted the highest number of refugees with 3.7 million, followed by Colombia with 1.7 million.

▼ **SOURCE A** Syrian children at a refugee camp in Adana, Türkiye, 2016.

Big Question

Migration words

There are lots of different words used to describe people who migrate. It is really important that you understand what is meant when you read or hear key terms such as migration, migrants, refugees and so on. They don't all mean exactly the same thing!

- People who move into a country are often called **immigrants**, while those who move out of a country are usually known as **emigrants**. In this book, we have generally referred to people as 'migrants'. Someone is an emigrant when they leave their place of residence and an immigrant when they arrive in their new country or place. Whether someone is referred to as an immigrant or an emigrant depends on the location of the people talking about them! Let's imagine a woman from the UK called Casey, who decides to move to Australia to live. People in the UK would refer to Casey as an emigrant (because she has left the place where these people live). People in Australia would refer to Casey as an immigrant (because she has come to the place these people live).
- Migration: the movement of a person or people from one country or place of residence to settle in another.
- Migrant: a person who moves away from their usual place of residence to another. This can be temporary or permanent, and for a variety of reasons. Sometimes the words 'immigrant' and 'emigrant' are used.
- Refugees: the terms 'migrants' and 'refugees' are often used interchangeably but it is important to know that there is a legal difference. Refugees are people who have been forced to leave their homes to escape war, persecution or a natural disaster. They will have had no choice but to leave and seek safety outside their country because their own government cannot (or will not) protect them. Refugees have a right to international protection.
- **Asylum seeker**: a person who has asked a government to recognise their status as a refugee and is waiting to hear the outcome of their application so they can be legally recognised as a refugee. Seeking asylum is a human right.

Key Words

migration   migrant   persecution
refugee   immigrant   emigrant   asylum seeker

▼ **SOURCE B** Adapted from a 2022 interview with 13-year-old Arsienii and his mother, Jane. Along with Arsienii's 8-year-old sister (Sofiia), they fled Ukraine after Russian forces invaded in early 2022. They arrived in the UK under the Homes for Ukraine scheme and were paired with a family based in Surrey, who offered to host them.

Arsienii: 'Is there anything you want people to know about refugees?'

Jane: 'Yes. At first, don't be like me and don't be a judge. Don't think that you know their situation. You have no idea how they feel or which life they live.'

Arsienii: 'How did our life change when the war started?'

Jane: 'It changed completely. We stopped being able to go to work, to go to school; we stopped being able to go to the shop to get fresh bread. Our life started to be dangerous and scary. I don't wish this change on anyone.'

Arsienii: 'Me too.'

[...]

Jane: 'What was leaving home like for you?'

Arsienii: 'Hard, because my friends stayed, my grandparents, and pets, my cat and my dog. But I tried to think that it's just a trip to London.'

Jane: 'A long trip.'

Over to You

1. In your own words, explain the difference between forced migration and voluntary migration. Give one example of each.
2. a What is an asylum seeker?
   b What is a refugee?
3. Read **Source B**.
   a Are Jane, Arsienii and Sofiia forced migrants or voluntary migrants?
   b Describe how their lives changed when the war started.

What is migration?

How do people migrate?

People migrate for all sorts of reasons, in all sorts of ways. Sometimes the government of a country might invite people because they are looking for specific skills or wanting to fill particular job vacancies. At other times there might be situations where the government decides to allow groups of people from a particular place to move there. This might be a result of war in their home country, for example. Look at the following examples of people who have migrated to the UK.

'I'm originally from Perth, Australia. I came to the UK to open a business. I took out a loan and opened a new coffee shop in Cambridge. Business is booming — and I employ lots of staff. I plan to open another coffee shop soon.'

'I arrived in the UK from the Caribbean in the 1950s when the UK government was encouraging migration to fill jobs in industries where there was a shortage of workers. I got a job as a nurse in London, and my uncle got a job with British Transport.'

'I fled from Somalia in East Africa in the late 1980s to escape a violent civil war. I was granted refugee status and settled in Birmingham. I had difficulty having the qualifications I gained in Somalia recognised in the UK, but have now worked my way up to a very responsible customer service job with a large insurance company.'

'In 1997, Hong Kong stopped being a British **colony** and became part of China. Around 50,000 people from Hong Kong were given British passports at this time, including me. I decided to move to the UK because there were some excellent job prospects in the banking and finance industries.'

'I am part of the Karen people, a minority ethnic group from Burma (now called Myanmar). In 1994, the Burmese (Myanma) government forced us from our homes, and we fled to a refugee camp in Thailand. We lived there for many years. I applied for resettlement, and my family and I were accepted by the UK. Now I live in Sheffield and I work as a care assistant. My son is at university and my daughter is a nurse.'

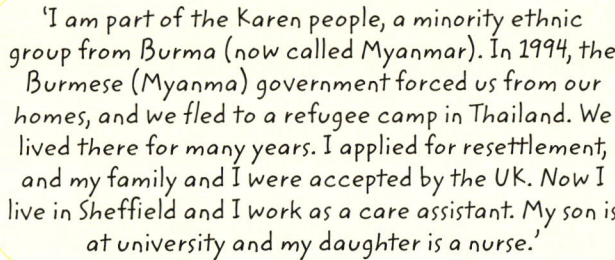

'I am one of a number of people who have applied for asylum in the UK because of my sexuality. In the country of my birth, it is illegal to be gay. In 2021, nearly 700 people were granted asylum in the UK in relation to their sexual orientation. This figure is 43 per cent higher compared to 2019.'

Modern slavery

Today, slavery is illegal in every country in the world. However, what is known as 'modern slavery' still exists. Modern slavery is when an individual is **exploited** by others, for personal reasons or to make money out of them. These people might be tricked or forced into losing their freedom.

Modern slavery might include the following – and each of these can involve moving to another country:

- Forced labour: as a result of threats and violence, people are transported to another place (even another country) to work in factories, pick crops, or serve food; some are forced into **prostitution**.
- Debt slavery: some people who live in poverty borrow money, but are forced to work to pay off the debt doing a job they don't want to do.
- Forced marriage: sometimes people, commonly children, are forced to marry someone against their will. They might be moved to another country to do this.

▶ **SOURCE A**
A poster from a 2017 government campaign to raise awareness of modern slavery in the UK.

Fact ✓

Figures from 2016 suggest that there could be between 10,000 and 13,000 victims of modern slavery in the UK. Many of these people are from Albania, Nigeria, Vietnam and Romania. It has been estimated that around 3,000 children from Vietnam alone are thought to be working in British cannabis farms and nail bars. They have been told their families will be hurt if they leave.

Big Question

Key Words

colony   exploited   prostitution

▼ **SOURCE B** From the website of the charity Anti-Slavery International.

'Why are people in slavery today?

People may end up trapped in slavery because they're vulnerable to being tricked, trapped and exploited, often as a result of poverty and exclusion and because laws do not properly protect them.

People can be particularly vulnerable to modern slavery when external circumstances push them into taking risky decisions in search of opportunities to provide for their families, or when people find they are simply pushed into jobs in exploitative conditions. Anyone could be pressed into forced labour, but people in vulnerable situations – such as being in debt, or not having access to their passport – are most at risk. Crises like the Covid-19 pandemic and climate change can make people even more vulnerable to exploitation.'

Over to You

1. Read each of the stories on page 10. For each person, note down:
   a. Did they migrate voluntarily or was it forced migration?
   b. Are they an economic migrant, refugee or asylum seeker?
   c. What was the reason they migrated?
2. Explain the meaning of the term 'modern slavery'.

Causation

Describe two reasons why people might be vulnerable to modern slavery.

Migration Nation

Big Question 2: Why should we study migration?

Migration is one of those topics that is always in the news. In fact, migration has been a 'hot topic' in this country for hundreds of years. Historians know that people, politicians and governments have always had strong opinions, debated, and argued over migration. It's fascinating to explore the experiences of, and challenges facing, different migrant groups throughout British history – and to see how the issues they faced were similar to and different from those of the people migrating today. So, what is it about Britain's migration story that makes its study so important?

Objectives
- Define key terms in relation to the story of migration in Britain.
- Examine reasons why the topic of migration should be studied.

Migration has made a huge impact

The impact of migration on Britain has been dramatic, influencing everything from the food we eat to the books we read and the freedoms we enjoy. Whether it's the Vikings from Scandinavia, Huguenots from France, Jewish people from Eastern Europe, or people from the Caribbean, the long history of migration to Britain has made an impact on many aspects of our lives today. Our high streets, cities and suburbs, hospitals, schools and sports teams, for example, have all been affected by the variety of cultural influences that are part of British society today as a result of migration in the past.

The study of migration is a window into the past

By studying the different groups of people who came to settle in Britain, we can learn about the different places they came from. But we learn even more about the country they came to, and the attitudes of the people who already lived in Britain at the time. How were different groups of migrants received? What problems did they face? What did they have in common? We can also learn about the contributions migrants have made in all areas of life.

Lots of history lessons cover the people who have the most power in society – the kings, queens and politicians, for example. The study of migration is about the history of people – why they moved, what their lives were like and how they have helped shape history.

SOURCE A From an article called *Beat the Backlash* written by the politician Barbara Roche in 2003.

> 'History should not be all about kings and queens, dates and battles, but should look at how immigration is firmly entwined with any notion of what it is to be British. Artistic, architectural and scientific legacies owe much to immigration.'

The migration story shows how Britain is connected to the world

British history is not just about what happens in Britain. It is important to show how Britain has influenced, and has been influenced by, the wider world. For example, from small beginnings in the early 1600s, Britain grew and grew. By 1900, Britain ruled over 400 million people living in 56 places all over the world. Many had been taught in school that Britain was the 'mother country' where they would always feel supported and welcome, even though this was not always the case. After the Second World War, citizens of the empire and Commonwealth had the right to settle in the UK. As a result, many people who were looking for new opportunities abroad chose Britain as a place to settle. Interestingly, today, of the top 20 countries of origin of foreign-born people in the UK, 12 of these places are former British colonies.

Big Question

Key Word Commonwealth empire

SOURCE B Jamaican men on the *Empire Windrush*, a ship carrying migrants to the UK in 1948. At the time, Jamaica was part of the British Empire.

Migration helps us discover hidden stories

The story of migration is a thoroughly absorbing one. It features some of the most remarkable events and people you could imagine. Also, it allows us to uncover some of the fascinating 'hidden' stories that might be unfamiliar to you – such as that of Sake Dean Mahomed, a South Asian migrant and entrepreneur. He opened an indoor bathhouse in Brighton in 1814 that offered a 'shampooing vapour medicated massage bath'. Before Mahomed came to Britain, British people would not have heard of the word 'shampoo'. Mahomed even became the 'shampooing surgeon' to both King George IV and King William IV.

Migration is an inclusive story

British society is a diverse, multicultural place. Some of you will have been born in other countries and moved to Britain, while others will have direct relatives (perhaps even parents or grandparents) who were born outside the UK. Almost certainly, everyone reading this now will have friends or classmates who have family links to India, or Pakistan, or Ireland, or Poland, for example.

It is important that everyone is included in history lessons. Young people should feel represented in the stories they learn about, the literature they read and so on. History lessons should represent the experiences of the people inside the classroom and the people who live in Britain. Migration, after all, is the story of all of us.

Over to You

Imagine you have told someone at home (a parent, carer, or sibling, for example) that you've just started the topic of migration in Britain at school. They have asked you, 'Why do you think your history teachers have chosen to teach you that?' In full sentences, write down what you would say in response.

SOURCE C Mahomed's Baths, Brighton, pictured in 1826. Mahomed promised his shampooing service was 'a cure to many diseases and giving full relief when everything fails; particularly rheumatic and paralytic, gout, stiff joints, old sprains, lame legs, aches and pains in the joints'.

Migration Nation

Big Question 3: Who were the earliest migrants to Britain?

We don't know much about the first people who lived in Britain. People didn't write things down at that time, so most of our information comes from evidence such as fragments of bone, tools, fossils, pottery and other artefacts. From these simple clues, experts have built up a basic picture of what life was like in Britain thousands of years ago. But who were some of the earliest migrants to Britain? Where did they come from, and why? And what impact did they have?

Objectives
- Describe Britain's early history before 1066.
- Examine the impact of different groups of invaders and settlers on Britain.

The very first migrants

It is thought that for hundreds of thousands of years, there were probably no humans in Britain at all – but there were animals. The sea level was a lot lower at that time, so these animals were able to walk across the floor of what is now the English Channel – a 'land bridge' that linked the British Isles to mainland Europe.

Then, about half a million years ago, people from Europe began to arrive. These were Britain's earliest migrants. They were **hunter-gatherers** who (as their name suggests) lived by gathering food (like nuts and fruit) and by killing animals for meat and furs. They moved around in small groups, and took shelter in caves or built basic huts. They learned skills such as lighting fires and making sharp flint tools.

▶ **INTERPRETATION A** This is an artist's idea of what historians think an early settlement from between 5000BCE and 4500BCE would look like. Most of the tools people used were made from wood and stone rather than iron or other metals – which is why this period is usually known as the Stone Age.

Britain and Europe move apart

For many thousands of years, during a period known as the Ice Age, hunter-gatherers could easily cross to Britain from Europe and back again across the land bridge where the English Channel now is. Then, around 8500BCE, the climate started to warm up and the ice began to melt. Over the next few thousand years, the land bridge gradually disappeared under water as the sea level rose, and Britain became an island.

More settlers

Life in Britain remained largely unchanged for thousands more years. More hunter-gatherers arrived from Europe by boat, and others left. Some fought with other groups while others stayed isolated. Around 7,000 years ago, an important change happened. People learned how to farm and produce their own food rather than having to hunt it and gather it. New settlers coming to Britain from Europe brought wheat and barley seeds to grow crops. They also brought animals for meat, including pigs, sheep and goats, and they owned tame dogs. They built more permanent homes and cleared large areas of woodland for farming (see **Interpretation A**).

▼ **SOURCE B** A house in the Stone Age village of Skara Brae in Orkney, Scotland. These houses were buried under sand dunes for thousands of years and only rediscovered after a storm in 1850. The area in the middle is the hearth, or fireplace. The sectioned-off areas to the side were beds. Historians think the shelves – or 'dresser' – were used to display special objects. Each house in Skara Brae has one of these.

▼ **SOURCE C** Stone Age tools, found in Essex, England.

The Bronze Age and Iron Age

Around 2500BCE, a new group of settlers began arriving in Britain from central Europe. Historians call them the Beaker people because of the decorated pottery they used. They knew how to make things out of metals like copper and gold. When tin was added to copper it made bronze, so the time of the Beaker people is often known as the Bronze Age. Soon, tools and weapons made from metal replaced the ones made from stone and wood. Around 800BCE, people learned how to make weapons and tools from iron. As a result, this period in British history is sometimes called the Iron Age.

Big Question

Key Word hunter-gatherer

The United Kingdom and Britain

In this book, we talk about the United Kingdom, Britain and England. This reflects the complicated history of these islands! Here is what each term means.

England	Before 1707, England and Wales were ruled as one country, separate from Scotland.
Britain	After 1707, England, Scotland and Wales were ruled together as Great Britain until the United Kingdom was formed in 1801 (see below). Great Britain is also used to refer to the biggest island of the British Isles.
United Kingdom (UK)	In 1801, Great Britain took control of the island of Ireland and became the United Kingdom. Most of Ireland separated from the United Kingdom in 1922, but Northern Ireland remains part of the United Kingdom.

Over to You

1. a. Why don't we know much about the people who first lived in Britain?
   b. How have historians tried to build up a picture of life back then?

2. a. Put the following periods in history into the correct chronological order:
   - Bronze Age
   - Iron Age
   - Stone Age

   b. How did each of these periods get its name?

3. In your own words, explain the terms 'England', 'Britain' and the 'United Kingdom'.

4. Look at **Interpretation A**. Work with a partner and discuss how the artist managed to create this picture. What evidence do you think they would have needed to make the image as accurate as possible?

Who were the earliest migrants to Britain?

After the Bronze Age

Over the next few thousand years, different tribes arrived in Britain. Some came peacefully, while others were hostile. Some came for only a short time, but others settled for good. Study each group carefully, thinking about how each one helped to shape Britain.

The Celts

Around 500 BCE, Celtic tribes from Europe arrived. The tribes fought brutally with each other, and with the people already settled in Britain.

- The Celts were proud of their appearance and kept themselves clean using special soaps and perfumes.
- They farmed the land and built forts.
- Priests (druids) led religious rituals. Some traditions survive today – Halloween and May Day have Celtic origins, for example.
- Tribal business was done at yearly assemblies: land disputes were settled, criminals were tried, and people were voted into important positions.

The Romans

The Romans, from Italy, invaded Britain in 43 CE and soon conquered many of the existing tribes in Britain. They stayed for around 400 years.

- Many of our roads are based on old Roman roads.
- Many Roman towns are still important today – for example, Chester, York, Bath, Lincoln, Colchester and St Albans.
- Many English words (such as 'peace' and 'street') and laws can be traced back to the Romans.
- The Romans who stayed in Britain were made up of diverse, multi-ethnic people including Gauls (from France), Germans, Hungarians and North Africans.
- Romans were the first in Britain to use calendars, coins and bricks, and they introduced peas, wine, grapes, carrots and cats.

Fact ✓

The Romans used the name 'Britannia' for Britain. This was based on 'Pretannia', which is what the Ancient Greeks called the British Isles because they thought a Celtic tribe called the 'Pretani' lived there. In fact, the Pretani tribe lived mainly in Ireland – but the name 'Pretannia' stuck, and later became Britannia, and then Britain.

Meanwhile... *400s BCE*

At this time, a variety of tribes (called Picts, Scotti, Britons and Angles) lived in what we now call Scotland. The Picts were the largest tribe – but it was the Scotti that the country was named after!

The Anglo-Saxons

In about 410 CE, the Romans returned to Italy to defend their homeland from invasion. The British people (now known as Britons) were left to fend for themselves, and it didn't take long for new tribes to invade. These tribes, from modern-day Denmark and northern Germany, were called Angles, Saxons and Jutes. Collectively, the invaders became known as Anglo-Saxons.

- The Anglo-Saxons drove many of the remaining British tribes into Wales, Cornwall, Cumbria and Scotland.
- Before converting to Christianity, they worshipped many gods. Some can be seen in our days of the week:
  - Tiw (god of combat) = Tuesday
  - Woden (god of war and wisdom) = Wednesday
  - Thor (protector of mankind) = Thursday
  - Freya (goddess of love and beauty) = Friday.
- Anglo-Saxon is one of the key 'base' languages of English – 'bed', 'cat', 'dog', 'tree', 'game', 'hunt' and 'fox' are all words of Anglo-Saxon origin.
- They gave England its name – 'Angle-land', meaning 'land of the Angles'; this later became 'England'.
- Many towns were created and named by Anglo-Saxons. If the name ends in '-ton', '-wich', '-worth', '-burn', '-hurst' or '-ham', Anglo-Saxons probably lived there.
- Lots of counties are named after the Anglo-Saxons. East Anglia is an obvious one. Another is 'Essex', the land of the East Saxons.
- They were excellent farmers.

Big Question

The Vikings

In the late eighth century the Anglo-Saxons faced invasion by Vikings who came across the North Sea from modern-day Denmark, Sweden and Norway. At the time, most Anglo-Saxons referred to these invaders as 'Danes' (Viking means 'raider' in the language of the Danes). At first, Vikings raided the coast: they stole valuable treasures, like gold, jewels and books. They also took food, cattle, clothes and tools. In 865CE, Vikings began to settle in Britain, rather than just raid it and return to their homelands. They knew that Britain had treasures that could make them rich, and fertile land for farming.

- There were many battles between Anglo-Saxons and Vikings. Gradually, Vikings took control of most of the large Anglo-Saxon kingdoms.
- For a time, the country was split into two – Anglo-Saxon lands in the south and west and Viking lands in the north and east.
- After many years of fighting and arguments between the two sides, Anglo-Saxons and Vikings became neighbours and there were many years of peace.
- By the mid-1000s, the country was united under one king, Edward the Confessor. His father had been an Anglo-Saxon king and his mother had once been married to a Viking king.

The Normans

In 1066, Normans (from Normandy, a region of France) invaded England and conquered the existing population.

- Normans controlled England and Wales (but failed to take over Scotland and most of Ireland).
- They built many fine castles, churches and cathedrals that still stand today.
- Over 10,000 words in our dictionaries come from these French settlers – for example: royal, city, soldier, parliament and prince.
- Names like William, Stephen, Emma, Henry, Alice, Matilda and Robert were introduced by them – and they invented surnames!
- They introduced deer, pheasants and rabbits – and planted the New Forest to hunt them in.
- Normans introduced many new laws, traditions and customs that are still in use today.

Fact ✓

The British Isles (the correct term for the islands that make up most of what people call 'Britain') lie off the north-west corner of mainland Europe. Incredibly, there are over 5,000 islands that make up the British Isles, but fewer than 200 of these are inhabited. The two largest islands – Great Britain and Ireland – have the most people living there, but other smaller islands – such as the Isle of Wight, Anglesey, Jersey, the Shetland Islands, the Orkney Islands and the Isle of Man – have lots of people living there too.

Over to You

1. a Explain how Britain got its name.
   b Explain how England and Scotland got their names.

2. Write two short paragraphs to answer the question: 'What did invaders and settlers bring to Britain?'

   Make sure you include the contribution and impact of the different groups of settlers – Celts, Romans, Anglo-Saxons, Vikings and Normans.

Consequence ⭐

Explain two consequences of the Roman invasion of Britain.

Migration Nation

1.1 The first Jewish community in England

After William won the Battle of Hastings in 1066 and became England's king, lots of people from France migrated to England. Among others, the new king encouraged Jewish merchants to settle, and to help build trade and wealth. From the late eleventh century onwards, the Jewish community was an important part of the English economy. However, just over 200 years later, all Jews were expelled from England after years of severe **persecution**. This chapter looks at how Jews helped build England's economy, why they were expelled in 1290, and who invited them back. It considers how Jews continued to settle in Britain and become an essential part of Britain's migration story.

Objectives

- Describe why Jews migrated to England in the medieval period.
- Examine the actions of medieval monarchs and the Catholic Church towards Jews.

Reasons for Jewish migration

There are no records of Jews in England before 1066 but, by 1100, there was a Jewish community of around 3,000 in the country. William the Conqueror invited Jews from Normandy to come to England to provide money for funding large-scale building projects (such as castles). This is because Jews, unlike Christians, were allowed to lend money to people and charge interest, which is a fee on top of money that is lent to someone. Christianity taught that it was a sin to charge interest. However, Judaism did not have the same restrictions.

Lots of people borrowed money from Jewish lenders of finance, including monarchs, merchants, church leaders and landowners. This was good for the country. Being able to borrow money enabled merchants to expand their businesses and increase trade which, in turn, meant the monarch could collect more taxes. Being able to borrow money also allowed landowners and monarchs to build cathedrals and castles, which brought prestige and power to the places they were built.

The experience of Jews

The monarch had personally invited Jewish people over to England from his lands in Normandy, and this meant that they were under his personal protection – but there were restrictions in place. For example, Jews were banned from a great number of jobs and could not own land. They also had to pay special taxes to the King. Nevertheless, large Jewish communities grew up in important towns such as London, Norwich, Lincoln, Bristol, Cambridge, Canterbury, Gloucester, Nottingham and Oxford. Medieval English Jews spoke mostly French, as did the monarchs and the aristocracy. They also spoke English, and wrote in Hebrew and Latin. They lived side-by-side with their Christian neighbours.

▶ **SOURCE A** The 'Jew's House' and 'Jews' Court' in Lincoln, two of the oldest surviving stone buildings in England, built around 1170. They were part of Lincoln's thriving medieval Jewish community. The last medieval Jewish owner of the Jew's House, before Jews were expelled from England in 1290, is believed to have been Belaset, daughter of Solomon of Wallingford.

Resentment, mistrust and persecution

English Jews may have had royal protection, but the Catholic Church went to great lengths to stir up hatred against them. In 1218, under pressure from the Catholic Church, England passed a law that required Jews to wear a special badge, although to begin with this was not widely enforced. In 1253, when the King needed money from the Church, the wearing of the badge was enforced, and the King commanded that Jews also had to pay taxes to the Church.

During the medieval period, Jews were often falsely accused of murdering Christian children as part of a ritual. This accusation is known as 'blood libel' and it first appeared in 1144 in Norwich. The Church encouraged and helped to spread these false accusations. In 1255, 18 Jews from Lincoln were hanged after being falsely accused of murdering a Christian boy.

Antisemitism increased in England during the Crusades. These were a series of journeys made by Christian Europeans to 'take back' the Holy Land, including Jerusalem, which was then ruled by Muslims. Many Christians did not see a difference between Muslims and Jews and this led to increasing attacks on Jewish communities. For example, in 1190 almost the whole of York's Jewish community was killed at Clifford's Tower at York Castle.

The end of royal protection

Gradually, Jews in Britain began to lose their royal protection and antisemitism worsened. Some kings, such as Henry III (reigned 1216–1272), fined or taxed the Jewish community heavily. One Jewish person – Abraham of Bristol – refused to pay one of the fines, so the king ordered that he have a tooth removed every day until he paid. Seven of his teeth were pulled out before Abraham gave in and paid.

In the late 1200s, royal protection for Jews in Britain came to an end. There were around 5,000 Jewish people in England at this time, out of a population of around three million. In 1275, Edward I passed a law that banned Jews from lending money. As they were also banned from doing many other jobs, many chose to leave the country. Those that remained had to wear a yellow patch of cloth on their clothes, so people knew they were Jewish. Some chose to convert to Christianity.

Fact

During one ten-year period in the 1200s, the Jewish communities of England were fined and taxed a total of £420,000 – that's over £220 million in today's money.

Key Words

persecution   antisemitism

Soon afterwards, Jews were banned from worshipping God in their own way – even in their own homes. Eventually, in 1290, Edward issued a royal decree and expelled Jews from England, seizing their land and property. He needed permission from Parliament to raise taxes to pay for war, and Parliament gave him this permission in exchange for expelling Jews from the country. It would be over 300 years before Jews were allowed to live in England again.

▼ **SOURCE B** An image of Jews being beaten, from a thirteenth-century English manuscript. The figures in blue and yellow are wearing a badge in the shape of two tablets. This makes it easier for them to be identified as Jews and persecuted. Notice the similarities with Nazi Germany's treatment of Jewish people.

Over to You

1. Explain why William the Conqueror invited Jewish people to England.

2. Look at **Source B**. What does this source reveal about attitudes towards Jews in thirteenth-century England?

3. a. What is meant by the word 'tolerant'?
   b. Was medieval England tolerant towards Jews? Write a paragraph explaining your answer.

Causation

Explain why Jews were expelled from England in 1290.

Migration Nation

1.2 The return of Jewish people

Jewish people had been expelled from England by King Edward I in 1290. In December 1655, a conference of English merchants, lawyers, and military and religious leaders concluded that 'there is no law against their [Jews] coming'. They decided that Jews had originally been expelled by a royal decree, and not by an official action by Parliament. This meant that the expulsion was a personal decision by Edward I, and not a law of the country. As a result, Jewish people were allowed to live in England. What happened next? Where did Jewish people settle? What contribution did Jewish people make to society?

Objectives

- Explain why Jewish people returned to Britain.
- Describe the treatment of nineteenth-century Jewish migrants to Britain.
- Examine their contribution to British society after their return.

New Jewish communities

Jews first settled in Aldgate in London, building a small **synagogue** within a year. As more Jews arrived, this area became home to a large Jewish community. By 1700, the Jewish population in England had grown to around 5,000 people, mainly in London, and by 1750 there were small Jewish communities in Liverpool, Hull and Portsmouth.

Jewish workers often worked in finance or in trades such as **peddling**, shopkeeping, shoe and furniture making or tailoring. As in the medieval period they faced restrictions. For example, Jews were not allowed to join the army, go to university or become lawyers.

British Jews

By the 1850s, the Jewish population of Britain had reached about 40,000 (in a population of 18 million). Over half of the Jewish population lived in London. The vast majority were integrated into British society. This meant that they had adopted many of the values and behaviours of the existing population, and spoke English. The first Jewish Mayor of London took office in 1855 and shortly afterwards Lionel de Rothschild became the first Jewish MP. Since then, the British Parliament has never been without politicians of Jewish heritage.

New arrivals

In the late nineteenth century, many Jewish migrants arrived in Britain. Most came from Eastern Europe and Russia, escaping poverty and **pogroms** (the organised killing of a particular ethnic group).

Most of the Jewish migrants who arrived were very poor. As a result, they had no choice but to settle in the poorest areas of large cities, where housing rents were cheaper. These places already had small Jewish communities, which the new migrants hoped would welcome them. Most of the new migrants were unable to speak English and were unable to work on the Jewish Sabbath

▶ **SOURCE A**
An engraving of Wentworth Street, Whitechapel, a poor area of London, 1872. It shows not only Jews, but other migrants – Irish, Indians and Germans, for example.

(from sunset on Friday evening until sunset on Saturday evening). As a consequence, it was almost impossible for them to get work with British employers. So, most found work with Jewish tailors making clothes, hats and shoes in small back-street workshops, known as sweatshops. There were around a thousand of these cramped, unhygienic and often dangerous sweatshops in London's East End.

▼ **SOURCE B** Mrs Brewer, a middle-class visitor to the East End of London, describing a visit to Spitalfields (where a large Jewish community lived) in the *Sunday Magazine* in 1892.

'My first impression on going among them was that I must be in some far-off country whose people and language I knew not. The names over the shops were foreign, the wares were advertised in an unknown tongue, of which I did not even know the letters […] when I addressed them in English the majority of them shook their heads.'

Some Jewish people who had been settled in Britain for generations took positive action to help the new migrants. For example, in 1885, a group of wealthy British Jews (known as the Four Percent Industrial Dwellings Company) built a series of good-quality blocks of flats in London. Another group, the Jewish Board of Guardians, lent money to help the very poor buy food and tools, such as sewing machines, that might help them find work. However, the Board of Guardians was worried that too many new Jewish migrants could cause problems for existing Jews in Britain. As a result, it organised for up to 50,000 recent Jewish migrants to be returned to their country of origin, or resettled elsewhere, mainly in the USA.

Not everyone treated the Jewish migrants kindly. They were accused of taking jobs from British people, and one newspaper campaigned against what it called the 'foreign flood' of migrants. In 1901, a group called the British Brothers' League was founded to campaign against immigration. The group claimed 45,000 members and organised mass meetings and protests. The negativity surrounding the Jewish migrants led to a law, the Aliens Act (1905), which restricted immigration of so-called 'undesirable immigrants'. This was the first law of its kind for a century. The Act also defined and allowed in refugees, but in practice this was often ignored.

Key Words

synagogue peddling pogrom sweatshop refugee

Success stories

Some of the new migrants set up successful businesses. Michael Marks, for example, arrived in Britain in 1882, escaping persecution in modern-day Belarus. He opened a market stall in 1884 and, in 1894, teamed up with Tom Spencer. By 1900, Marks and Spencer had 36 outlets, and it is now one of the best-known high street stores in the world. Jack Cohen, the son of Polish Jewish immigrants, set up a business in Hackney in London selling (among other things) tea from a supplier called T.E. Stockwell. He soon made a brand name for his business by using part of his surname and the initials of his main supplier – TESCO!

▶ **SOURCE C** Michael Marks, founder of Marks and Spencer.

Over to You

1 a For what reasons did large numbers of Jews arrive in Britain in the 1870s and 1880s?
   b Describe how the 'new arrivals' were treated.
   c Suggest reasons why the new Jewish immigrants were treated this way.

2 Look closely at **Source A**. First, describe what you see. Then try to explain what you think the artist thought about immigrants.

3 Write a sentence or two explaining how each of the following organisations and people links to the story of Jewish migration in the nineteenth century:
   • Four Percent Industrial Dwellings Company
   • Jewish Board of Guardians
   • British Brothers' League
   • Michael Marks and Jack Cohen

1.3 The Battle of Cable Street

On 4 October 1936, in a poor area of the East End of London, women could be seen throwing milk bottles at policemen. Children dropped marbles under the hooves of police horses and burst bags of pepper in front of their noses. People built barricades from paving stones, fence posts and overturned lorries. These people, mainly poor Jewish residents, were helped by dockworkers and trade-unionists. Their aim was to stop a political march through the streets of a mainly Jewish area of London. The police became targets because they were there to clear a path through the streets for the marchers. This confrontation became known as the Battle of Cable Street. So what was the political march about? Why did the march go through a Jewish area? And what has this confrontation got to do with the story of migration?

Objectives

- Describe the treatment of Jews in Europe.
- Examine the British response to Jewish refugees.

Antisemitism in Germany

In Germany, in the 1930s, Adolf Hitler's Nazi Party introduced many antisemitic laws designed to make life so unpleasant for Jews that they would choose to leave Germany. For example, severe restrictions were placed on everyday life and Jewish business owners were forced to hand their businesses to the state.

Many Jewish people left Germany before the outbreak of the Second World War, to escape this persecution, and settled in nearby countries. Between 1933 and 1939, 80,000 Jewish people came to Britain as refugees.

British Nazis

In Britain at this time, there was a political party with many views similar to those of the Nazi Party in Germany. It was called the British Union of Fascists (BUF), also known as the Black Shirts because of their uniform. It was led by Oswald Mosley, and he had grown popular with some British people because of his views on, among other things, migration. During this time many people in Britain were without jobs and Mosley argued that migrants took the jobs of British workers. Like Hitler in Germany, he directed his hatred towards the Jewish community. By 1934, the BUF had around 40,000 members, and at meetings they gave the Nazi salute and chanted 'Hail Mosley' and 'Down with Jews'.

▶ **SOURCE A**
Oswald Mosley, leader of the BUF, in London in 1934.

Political marches

It was common for the BUF to go on marches through city centres. These were always followed by a speech by Mosley. Marches were a way of showing the party's strength and organisation, as well as a chance to get its message across to a wider audience.

On Sunday 4 October 1936, Mosley planned to send thousands of his supporters into the East End of London dressed in uniforms similar to those of Hitler's Nazis. The area was full of poor workers, and had a large Jewish community.

The Battle of Cable Street

When news got out of the BUF's march, a crowd of up to a quarter of a million people gathered to block the route. The police arrived too, and tried to clear a way for the BUF. At the time, political marches like this were legal, and so the police were doing their job of ensuring the rights of a political group to march freely. But the crowd had other ideas.

At around 3:00pm the marchers reached Cable Street – and were stopped! They waited for the police to clear a path through the crowd, but it was impossible. Soon the police and some members of the crowd clashed. Barricades of old mattresses, a broken-down lorry and broken paving stones appeared. The police were bombarded with missiles from the crowd and banners appeared that read, 'They shall not pass'.

After an unsuccessful hour or so, the police left and the BUF marched around the Jewish area and headed for the centre of London. The marchers put up racist posters and smashed Jewish shop windows as they went.

▼ **INTERPRETATION B** Adapted from an interview with eyewitness Bill Fishman, a British historian who was born in London in 1921. He was the son of two migrants, one from Ukraine and one from Russia. Quoted in a 2006 *The Guardian* newspaper online article by Audrey Gillan.

'Suddenly a barricade was erected there and they put an old lorry in the middle of the road and old mattresses [...] We were all side by side. I was moved to tears to see bearded Jews and Irish Catholic dockers standing up to stop Mosley. I shall never forget that as long as I live, how working-class people could get together to oppose the evil of racism.'

▼ **SOURCE C** A photograph taken during the Battle of Cable Street, 4 October 1936.

Key Words

trade-unionists   antisemitic   interned

The aftermath

The BUF was furious that the march had been disrupted. In the weeks that followed, it stepped up its antisemitic campaign. There was also further violence. The Sunday after the Battle of Cable Street, a mob of around 200 people took to the streets of nearby Mile End, attacking Jews, smashing Jewish shop windows, and shouting anti-Jewish slogans. This became known as the Mile End Pogrom.

However, after the Battle of Cable Street, the government gave the police the right to ban political marches like the one that took place in the East End that day, and it also banned the wearing of political uniforms in public. Support for Mosley began to die down. In 1940, after the outbreak of the Second World War and when Britain was at war with Hitler's Germany, the BUF was disbanded, and Mosley interned.

Over to You

1. Describe the persecution Jews faced in Europe in the 1930s.

2. a. What was the BUF?
   b. Why do you think the BUF chose the East End of London for its march on 4 October 1936?
   c. Why did the police become targets of violence during the Battle of Cable Street?

3. The BUF was prevented from marching down Cable Street but it still marched into the centre of London, smashed Jewish shop windows and put up racist posters. Who, in your opinion, 'won' the Battle of Cable Street?

Source Analysis

How useful is **Source C** for a historian studying the Battle of Cable Street? Explain your answer using the source and your own knowledge.

Migration Nation 23

1.4 Jewish people in modern Britain

Look at **Source A**. It is a photograph of a bronze memorial, called *Kindertransport – The Arrival*, and it is located just outside Liverpool Street railway station in London. It commemorates the 10,000 Jewish children who escaped Nazi persecution and arrived at the station between December 1938 and September 1939. What exactly was the Kindertransport scheme? How many Jewish refugees arrived during the Second World War? What has been the story of Jewish people in Britain since then?

Objectives

- Examine the British response to Jewish refugees during the Second World War.
- Explore the development of the Jewish community and Jewish life in modern Britain.

▶ **SOURCE A** *Kindertransport – The Arrival* at Liverpool Street Station, London.

▼ **SOURCE B** An account by Mariam Cohen from Norwich, England. She fostered a child who arrived in Britain as part of the Kindertransport.

'I remember motoring to Norwich to pick up Kurt [...] We saw a ship coming in, and then we saw these poor little things straggling off the gangplank. They had been sick, and were dirty, and they smelled of ship and seasickness. And we brought them home [...] My mother, bless her, she took a little girl, Elizabeth, whose family used to phone every Friday night from Vienna [Austria]. One Friday night, there was no phone call, and poor little girl, she knew what it was. She sat in that little grandmother's chair and she covered her head with a shawl, and she just sobbed and sobbed.'

Kindertransport

Kindertransport (which means 'children's transport' in German) was the organised rescue of children from Nazi-controlled territory. It took place in the months before the outbreak of the Second World War in September 1939. Most children came from Germany, Austria, the former Czechoslovakia and Poland. The children were allowed to enter Britain without visas or passports, and were placed in foster homes, in schools and on farms.

The children's parents were not allowed to accompany them to Britain. The Kindertransport scheme stopped in September 1939 when war broke out and countries closed their borders. In many cases, the children were the only members of their families to survive the Holocaust. After the Second World War, many Jewish refugees stayed in Britain. Many also moved to Israel and the USA.

▶ **SOURCE C** The official documents, from 1939, that allowed these three children to escape to Britain from Austria as part of the Kindertransport scheme.

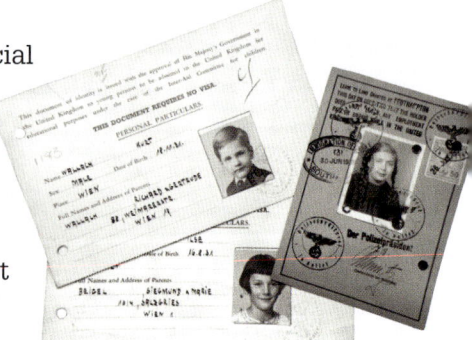

Jewish refugees

Before war broke out in 1939, around 80,000 Jewish refugees arrived in Britain, mostly on temporary visas. Many British people were worried about the number of refugees arriving because they were concerned there would be competition for jobs and housing. However, when news of the Nazi persecution of Jewish people became known people became more welcoming.

Chapter 1: Jewish migration

Jewish life in Britain today

In the years after the war, many Jewish people began to move away from the mainly Jewish communities in city centres and out into the suburbs. Today, Jewish people live all over Britain, but there are particularly large communities in London, Manchester, Leeds and Glasgow. Approximately two thirds of Britain's 300,000 Jews live in London.

British Jews today are a very diverse group of people. Jewish people are represented in all walks of life, professions and occupations. Not all Jews worship in the same way – and not all Jews are religious. For some people, their Jewish ancestry is the main reason they identify as Jewish. For others, it is because of the religious practices they follow. There are around 450 synagogues in the UK, with around three quarters of British Jews belonging to a synagogue. In a recent study, when asked to explain their Jewish identity, the most common answer was 'just Jewish'. Find out about some well-known British Jews in **Sources D–F**.

▶ **SOURCE D** Ernst Chain was a German-born Jewish biochemist best known for his work (with Australian Howard Florey) on the development of penicillin, the first antibiotic. Chain fled from Nazi Germany in 1933 and migrated to the UK.

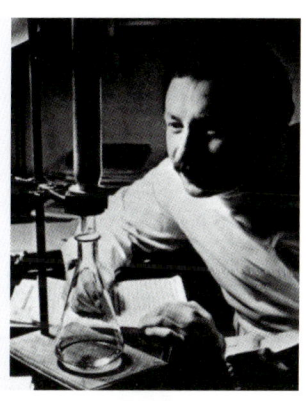

▶ **SOURCE E** Michael Rosen is a British children's author, poet, broadcaster and activist, born into a Jewish family. He has written over 100 books including *We're Going on a Bear Hunt* and *The Bus is for Us*.

▶ **SOURCE F** Claudia Winkleman, born in London to a Jewish family, is a British television presenter and journalist. She is perhaps best known as a presenter of the dance contest show *Strictly Come Dancing*.

Key Words
Holocaust

Fact

Antisemitism is still an issue in Britain today and has been on the rise in recent years, with Jewish people experiencing physical and verbal attacks. In 2018, for example, around 30 headstones at a Jewish cemetery in Manchester were smashed. In fact, more antisemitic incidents were recorded in the UK in 2021 than in any year since 1984, when the recording of these incidents began.

▼ **SOURCE G** Vandalised headstone at a Jewish cemetery in Manchester, 2016.

Over to You

1. Look at **Source A**.
   a. Describe the statue.
   b. Why do you think the statue was built at Liverpool Street railway station in London?

2. Using **Sources A, B and C**, and your own knowledge, write a paragraph about the Kindertransport. Make sure you:
   - define Kindertransport
   - explain why the scheme was necessary.

3. Look at **Source G**. How useful is this source to a historian studying Jewish life in modern Britain?

Source Analysis

How could you follow up **Source B** to find out more about the Kindertransport system?

In your answer, you must give the question you would ask and the type of source you could use.

Note down:
- detail in **Source B** that I would follow up
- question I would ask
- what type of source I could use
- how this might help answer my question.

Migration Nation 25

1 Have you been learning?

🔄 Quick Knowledge Quiz

Choose the correct answer from the three options:

1. Which King invited Jews to migrate to England in the eleventh century?
   a. Harold of Wessex
   b. William the Conqueror
   c. Edward I

2. In the thirteenth century, a new law was made which said English Jews had to do what to show that they were Jewish?
   a. wear special clothes
   b. wear a patch of yellow cloth
   c. put a sign on their front door

3. In what year were Jews expelled from England?
   a. 1190
   b. 1290
   c. 1390

4. In what century were Jews allowed to return to England?
   a. seventeenth century
   b. eighteenth century
   c. nineteenth century

5. During the nineteenth century, many Jews arrived in the UK, fleeing persecution. Where did they migrate from?
   a. Spain and Portugal
   b. Russia and Eastern Europe
   c. India

6. These Jews were often poor and worked in very crowded, backstreet workshops. What were these workshops known as?
   a. studios
   b. sweatshops
   c. labour rooms

7. Which British companies were founded by Jewish migrants and their descendents?
   a. Sainsbury's and WHSmith
   b. Ford and Cadbury's
   c. Marks and Spencer and Tesco

8. The Battle of Cable Street in 1936 took place when (mainly Jewish) people tried to prevent a Fascist march passing through their area. In which city did it take place?
   a. London
   b. Manchester
   c. Liverpool

9. What was the Kindertransport?
   a. an organised rescue scheme for Jewish families fleeing Nazi persecution in Europe
   b. a ship carrying Jewish refugees fleeing Nazi persecution
   c. an organised rescue scheme for Jewish children in Nazi-occupied Europe

10. Approximately how many Jewish people live in the UK today?
    a. 1 million
    b. 500,000
    c. 300,000

Have you been learning?

Analysing cartoons

For centuries, political cartoons have appeared in newspapers and magazines. A political cartoon is a cartoon that makes a point about a political issue or event. They can sometimes be funny, but their main purpose is to get you thinking carefully (and, perhaps, differently) about a particular event or issue – and to try to sway your opinion toward the cartoonist's ideas or point of view.

Look at the political cartoon in **Source A** carefully.

▼ **SOURCE A** A cartoon published in 1905 after the introduction of the Aliens Act (1905). It comments on the changing attitudes to migrants to Britain.

"Britannia: I can no longer offer shelter to fugitives. England is not a free country".

1. What was the Aliens Act (1905)? Perhaps look at page 21 to remind you.
2. Why had there been an increase in migration in the years leading up to the publication of this cartoon?
3. Which country is represented by the woman on the left?
4. Do you think the cartoonist supports the Aliens Act? Why or why not?

Defining key words and terms

As a historian, it is important that you can quickly recognise and define key terms and words. You should also be able to describe them at length.

1. Complete the sentences below with an accurate term.
   - After 1066, Jewish merchants were encouraged to settle in England by…
   - King Edward I expelled Jewish people from England in 1290. He was given permission by…
   - Jewish people began to return to England after…
   - By 1700, the Jewish population in England had grown to around 5,000 people, mainly in…

2. Write two definitions for each of the words, terms, events and people listed below.
   a. For the first one, use no more than ten words.
   b. The second definition can be more detailed, using up to 30 words.

   The first one has been done for you:
   - persecution:
     a. The bad treatment of an individual or group of people. (10 words)
     b. The unfair or cruel treatment of someone, or a group of people, over a long period because of their race, religion, political beliefs or some other difference. (27 words)

   - British Brothers' League
   - British Union of Fascists
   - Battle of Cable Street
   - Kindertransport

Migration Nation

Big Question 4: Why have migrants come to Britain?

In 1066, the Normans (led by William the Conqueror) invaded England, conquered it, and stayed for good. Since this Norman invasion, no other foreign power has invaded and taken over. However, lots of different migrant groups have come to Britain and made it their home. Who are some of the groups? Why did they come?

Objectives
- Examine several migrant groups that arrived in Britain in the years since 1066.

Fact ✓
People don't just come to live in Britain – they leave Britain too. British people have emigrated for all sorts of reasons – including a better job, a better climate or more opportunities. Most people will know someone who has emigrated to another country, perhaps to retire or because they have a job offer. In 2020, for example, 268,000 people came to settle in Britain … and 234,000 people left Britain to live abroad.

In the 1500s, groups of migrants from the Low Countries (modern-day Belgium, the Netherlands and Luxembourg) began to settle in England, mainly in London, Norwich, Sandwich and Canterbury. Known as Flemish and Walloon migrants, they came to England to escape religious persecution. The migrants were highly skilled silk-weavers who set up new businesses, provided jobs for people, and passed on their weaving skills to local craftspeople.

▼ **SOURCE A** Silk is made from the cocoons of silkworms. This seventeenth-century illustration shows Flemish women unwinding cocoons and preparing the silk for weaving.

In the late 1500s and 1600s, large numbers of French Protestants came to England. These migrants, known as Huguenots, were fleeing religious persecution in France. Many Huguenots set up successful businesses and brought new skills and techniques to Britain. These included improved methods of making glass, watches, clocks, spectacles, hats, wigs, silk and fine paper (which made the printing of paper money possible). They even set up their own charity organisations (called Friendly Societies) to help those among them who had fallen on hard times, an idea that was copied by English workers years later. In fact, some historians have said that the arrival of the Huguenots was one of the key reasons that Britain developed from a farming nation to a world-leading industrial nation in the 1800s. By 1800, Huguenots were about five per cent of London's population. It has been estimated that around three quarters of English people today have some Huguenot ancestry (including Prince William and his brother, Harry).

▶ **SOURCE B** A memorial at the Huguenot burial ground, London, England, erected in 1911. The memorial mentions the Edict of Nantes, in which the French king promised safety for Protestants. However, this was reversed and many Hugenots fled as a result.

Big Question

Fact ✓

The Bank of England was founded in 1694. Today it is the central bank of the United Kingdom and a very important institution. Its first governor was Sir John Houblon, the grandson of a Huguenot refugee.

Chinese sailors, working on British ships, began to arrive in Britain in the late 1700s. Some decided to settle and establish communities. These communities often became known as 'Chinatown', with the biggest in Liverpool and East London. Chinese businesspeople opened shops, restaurants and laundries. The first Chinese restaurant in Britain opened in London in 1908. In the 1950s and 1960s, there was further large-scale migration from China due to the repressive Communist government there.

Jewish people have settled in Britain for over a thousand years. First invited by William the Conqueror in 1066, they prospered as teachers, poets, doctors and lenders of finance. Jews were then expelled from England in 1290 but were allowed to return in the 1600s. By 1700, the Jewish population in England had grown to around 8,000 people, mainly in London, but there were also small Jewish communities in the ports of Liverpool, Hull and Portsmouth. In the late 1800s, large numbers of Jews arrived from Eastern Europe and Russia, escaping poverty and pogroms (the organised and deliberate killing of a particular ethnic group). Many quickly sailed off to start a new life in the USA, but approximately 150,000 stayed in Britain, mainly settling in places where there were existing Jewish communities, such as in London and Glasgow. Lots of Jewish people left Nazi Germany around the time of the Second World War too. Around 60,000 Jews settled in Britain at this time.

▼ **SOURCE D** Chinese seamen playing mahjong (a Chinese game), Liverpool, 1962.

▼ **SOURCE C** A fried fish shop in Petticoat Lane, East London, 1906. Fried fish was a dish brought to Britain by Jewish migrants.

Migration Nation

Why have migrants come to Britain?

Between 1871 and 1881, 750,000 people migrated from Italy to Britain. They were escaping the unrest that followed wars fought to free Italy from foreign control. Italian migrants moved in large numbers to London, South Wales and Glasgow. They brought many skills with them from Italy, developing a reputation for making ceramics and tiles, and making religious artefacts to sell door-to-door. They brought the Italian 'cafe culture' to Britain, and soon became known for making and selling ice cream. In Scotland, some Italians opened fish and chip shops; many fish and chip shops in Scottish towns and cities are still run by Italians today.

▼ **SOURCE E** Cafe Nardini in Largs, Scotland, opened in 1935 and serves 32 flavours of ice cream.

It is estimated that by the 1800s there were around 40,000 South Asians in Britain. They were mainly sailors (called lascars) who had decided to stay in Britain, but there were also ayahs (nannies and nursemaids for rich families), servants, students, officials, doctors and businesspeople. In the late 1940s, 1950s and 1960s, there was more large-scale migration from South Asia as people fled violence and looked for work and educational opportunities.

▼ **SOURCE G** Two ayahs from Madras (now Chennai), India, photographed in Glasgow, 1925.

There is a long history of Irish migration to Britain. However, large-scale migration occurred in the mid-1800s as a result of famine and the search for work building Britain's canals, roads and railways during the industrial revolution. There were further periods of Irish immigration in the 1930s, 1950s and 1960s – mostly people looking for work in Britain's expanding cities. Today, it is estimated that as many as six million people living in Britain have at least one Irish grandparent.

▶ **SOURCE F** The Royal Albert Dock is a huge complex of dock buildings and warehouses alongside the River Mersey in Liverpool. Many of the people who built the Albert Dock were Irish migrant labourers. When it opened in 1846 it was considered to be revolutionary in design because goods from ships were loaded and unloaded directly from the warehouses.

Big Question

Many South Asians came to Britain in the 1960s and 1970s. They had moved from India and Pakistan to the African nations of Kenya and Uganda when these nations were part of the British Empire – but now the newly independent Kenyan and Ugandan governments were driving them out. Around 44,000 Asians from Kenya and 26,000 from Uganda came to Britain at this time.

▼ **SOURCE H** Migrants at Stansted Airport after being forced to flee their homes in Uganda, 1972.

Around 15,000 people from the Caribbean settled in Britain after the First World War. During the Second World War thousands more moved to Britain to help with the war effort, although most returned home when the war ended. From the late 1940s to 1970, more migrants from places such as Jamaica, Barbados, and Trinidad and Tobago were encouraged to come to Britain because of a shortage of workers.

▼ **SOURCE J** Caribbean migrants arriving in Tilbury docks, London, 1948.

Migrants from Eastern European countries (such as Poland, Hungary, Romania and the Czech Republic) have been settling in Britain since at least the late 1500s. However, large-scale migration took place around the time of the Second World War as people fled conflict and persecution in their homelands. Thousands of Eastern Europeans joined Britain's armed forces to fight against Hitler's Germany. In more recent years, when Eastern European countries became part of the European Union, many Eastern Europeans migrated to Britain in search of work.

▼ **SOURCE I** A Polish shop in Hackney, London, 2010. Polish shops can be found all over the UK, catering to Polish and other Eastern European migrants who came to Britain after the expansion of the EU.

Over to You

Over the last four pages you have looked at several immigrant groups who have settled in Britain over the last 1,000 years – Jews, Huguenots, Irish people, Eastern Europeans, people from the Caribbean, Chinese people, South Asians and Kenyan and Ugandan Asians. Create a timeline showing when these different people and cultures came to Britain. When labelling your timeline, try to include details of the reasons they came to Britain (was it voluntary or forced migration, for example?) and one or two sentences saying what changes they brought about and/or what contributions they made to the British way of life. Top tip: this task is ideally suited to be done on A3 paper – and made bright and colourful for use as a class display.

Consequence

Describe two consequences of the Huguenots' migration to Britain.

Migration Nation

2.1 The Great Hunger

Today, it is estimated that as many as six million people living in Britain have at least one Irish grandparent. This is around ten per cent of the population. The 2021 census revealed that over half a million people living in Britain were born on the island of Ireland. But Irish migration is not a recent thing – people from Ireland have migrated to Britain for hundreds of years. This chapter explores the history of Irish migration – the reasons the migrants came, how people reacted to their arrival, and the impact they made, both at the time and continuing to this day.

> **Objectives**
> - Explain reasons why Irish immigrants came to Britain in the late 1700s and 1800s.
> - Examine the impact of the Great Hunger.

Early migration

Britain and the island of Ireland are close to each other. In fact, Ireland and Britain are just 20km apart at the Irish Sea's narrowest point! People from England and Scotland settled and colonised parts of Ireland from the twelfth century. In 1800, British politicians voted that the whole of Ireland should become part of Britain. On 1 January 1801, Great Britain and Ireland officially united to become the United Kingdom of Great Britain and Ireland. As a result, people have moved between the two places for centuries. Some British towns and cities, especially London, Bristol and Whitehaven (in Cumbria) had large communities of Irish traders as early as the 1650s, as well as lots of Irish workers on farms, especially at harvest time. Manchester had an Irish population of around 5,000 by the late 1700s, and around 30,000 Irish migrants lived in Liverpool by the early 1800s.

> **Fact** ✓
> Temporary migration from Ireland was also common. This meant that people would come to Britain for shorter stays, often to get a job during harvest time. In the summer of 1841, for example, 57,651 Irish labourers, mainly men, crossed to England and Scotland to work on the harvest.

Increasing Irish migration

There was an increase in Irish migration in the 1800s, mainly through the ports of Liverpool and Glasgow. Thousands stayed in those cities (and there are still large Irish communities there today) but others moved to other parts of Britain. Most came to escape extreme poverty in parts of Ireland, and to find better paid work. However, the number of Irish migrants rose dramatically in the mid-1800s when the potato crop failed catastrophically several years in a row.

> **Fact** ✓
> Irish soldiers were a major element of the British Army throughout the nineteenth century. In 1830, for example, around 40 per cent of soldiers in the British Army were Irish-born.

The Great Hunger

By the 1840s, around eight million people lived in Ireland. Most were poor peasants who rented tiny farms from landowners. A large number of these landowners were English, from families that had taken the land from the Irish many years before. Now the Irish had to rent land that had once belonged to them. The land was poor quality and the rents were high. Most of these peasants lived on nothing but the potatoes they grew in their fields. They couldn't even afford bread.

In September 1845, a disease called 'potato blight' started to destroy the Irish potato crop. Over the following years, Ireland lost between one third and one half of its potatoes. Millions of people were left without their main source of food. Between 1845 and 1851 around one million people (or one eighth of the Irish population) died, either from starvation or from illnesses that their weakened bodies couldn't fight. This event is known as the 'Great Hunger' or the 'Irish Potato Famine'.

Hundreds of thousands fled to Britain, peaking in the 1840s and 1850s, when over one and a half million Irish people left their homeland. These refugees tended to settle close to their port of entry, simply because their health was so poor and they had so little money that they couldn't travel far. This is why port cities such as Liverpool had large Irish communities. In fact, between 1844 and 1851, the proportion of Irish-born Liverpudlians went from about 17 per cent to 22 per cent.

By 1861, there were around 600,000 Irish-born people in Britain. Like many migrant groups, before or since, the Irish tended to live close together in towns and cities. Despite getting work, they were not wealthy, and often ended up in the poorest quality housing in the worst parts of town.

Meanwhile...

The British government (which controlled Ireland) did little to help the starving Irish people and, in fact, made the situation worse. For example, ships continued to take goods such as wheat, oats, barley, butter, peas, beans, fish and honey out of Ireland to sell overseas which profited the British landowners, but not the poor Irish farmers. But the Great Hunger was one of the first national disasters to provoke an international fund-raising campaign. People from India, America, Australia, Italy and France raised money to send to Ireland. The Choctaw Nation, a group of Indigenous Americans, sent over $170.

▼ **SOURCE A** A French cartoon of an 1849 visit to Ireland by Queen Victoria, during the Great Hunger. It shows the men who greeted her (probably English men who owned land in Ireland) covering up the starving population with their coats to hide them from view.

Later on...

In the 1800s, nearly one million Irish migrants travelled to the USA. Today, large communities with Irish ancestry can be found in many US cities including Philadelphia, Chicago and Boston. Many places across the country have annual St Patrick's Day parades; the one in New York is one of the world's largest parades.

▶ **SOURCE B** A statue built in 1998 to commemorate victims of the Great Hunger in Boston, USA.

Over to You

1 Define the 'Great Hunger'.
2 What was the impact of the famine?
3 Look at **Source A**.
   a Describe what is happening in the source.
   b Why do you think the men would want to cover up the queen's view?
   c This is a French cartoon. We are not sure this actually happened. Why then, do you think it was published?
4 Look at **Source B**. Why do you think there is a memorial to the Great Hunger in the USA?

Causation

Describe two causes of the Great Hunger.

2.2 How did Irish people help build Britain?

Irish people were one of the largest migrant groups to come to Britain in the eighteenth and nineteenth centuries. Hundreds of thousands came in the 1840s and 1850s when famine hit Ireland. Many others came to find work building canals and railways and working in factories and dockyards during the industrial revolution of the 1700s and 1800s.

Objectives

- Define 'navvies' and their impact on the industrial revolution.
- Analyse the reactions to Irish migration.

Navvies

Irish migrants got jobs in a number of different industries, including working in mines and in cotton mills. They contributed to the expansion of Britain's towns and cities and its overall industrial growth. Many Irish migrants found jobs all around the country as **navvies**, building canals, roads, railways and docks. In 1850, around a quarter of a million navvies were employed on the railways, and one third of these were Irish.

Building railways was hard, dangerous work that involved using gunpowder, picks and shovels to clear the way for the railway line. Navvies had a reputation for being strong and hard-working. Between 1839 and 1852, navvies built the Woodhead Tunnel under the Pennines between Sheffield and Manchester. The work was so dangerous that the navvies who built it suffered a higher death rate than the soldiers who fought at the Battle of Waterloo against Napoleon's army in 1815. The loss of life prompted an inquiry in Parliament but no action was taken for years.

In the early years, navvies had to travel with the railways as they were built, so they lived in makeshift huts next to the bridges, tunnels and cuttings they were building. They developed their own lifestyle and culture and gained a reputation for heavy drinking and fighting.

▼ **INTERPRETATION B** The historian J.E. Handley describes Irish migration to Britain in his book *The Irish in Scotland*, written in 1947. Although the book is about Scotland, his words apply to the whole of Britain.

'The coal, iron and textile industries attracted tens of thousands of immigrants in search of work [...] with expansion [of towns and cities] came the growth of the Irish population [...] The decline of linen and woollen industries in the north of Ireland and the rise of the cotton industry [in Britain] [...] attracted Irish towards the city [of Glasgow].'

Fact ✓

It is not true that all Irish migrants at the time were manual workers and poor. Many were, but there were also some middle-class migrants working as schoolteachers, midwives, shopkeepers and doctors.

▶ **SOURCE A**
This is an example of an early navvy hut. As time went on, the huts became more sophisticated with glass windows and even small gardens, although they were still simple buildings. Many navvies brought their families with them as they built the railways.

▶ **SOURCE C** The Royal Albert Dock is a huge complex of dock buildings and warehouses alongside the River Mersey in Liverpool. When it opened in 1846, it was considered revolutionary in design because goods from ships were loaded and unloaded directly from the warehouses. It was built by Irish navvies.

▼ **INTERPRETATION D** From an article called 'The Navvies: How the Irish built the modern British railways', published online in 2015 by history writer Matthew Calfe.

'Designers may have mapped the routes and engineers built the stock that would travel them, but these Irishmen had a large hand in blasting the routes for the tunnels, building the embankments and viaducts, and making the designs reality using nothing more than brute strength and explosives. These Irishmen were a key part in the building of modern Britain.'

How did the existing British population react to Irish migration?

CRIME
Irish migrants were blamed for high crime rates in many towns and cities. Many navvies tended to drink a lot of alcohol and this would sometimes lead to violence. Irish people were often used as scapegoats for crime more generally. In 1847, *The Times* newspaper described the Irish as 'more like squalid apes than human beings'.

RELIGIOUS DIFFERENCES
Most Irish migrants were Catholic – and Britain was a strongly Protestant country. Religious differences could lead to violence, and on several occasions angry Protestants marched through Irish areas and destroyed property.

Reaction to Irish migration

JOBS
Irish migrants were accused of taking jobs that the British could have done. There were anti-Irish protests: in some places people with Irish accents (or even Irish names) were barred from jobs. As a result, there were times when the Irish couldn't always find regular work – so they were accused of being lazy too.

DISEASE
Irish migrants often lived in terrible conditions so disease was common. As a result, people would blame the Irish for causing the disease in the first place. The fact that disease was just as common in other places seemed to go unnoticed. Typhus – a deadly infectious disease common in crowded, unsanitary conditions – was even nicknamed 'Irish fever'.

Key Words   navvies   scapegoat

Fact ✓

Irish-born Jewish immigrant Thomas Barnardo opened his first orphanage in London in 1870. As well as providing clothes, food and somewhere to sleep, it trained children in shoe-making, carpentry and metalwork. Within 30 years, nearly 60,000 children had been helped. Today, Barnardo's is one of the leading children's charities in Britain.

Over to You

1. Why did so many people leave Ireland in the late eighteenth and nineteenth centuries?

2. a. What was a navvy?
   b. Describe the life of a navvy.
   c. What point does the writer of **Interpretation D** make about Irish workers?

3. a. Make a list of all the problems blamed on the Irish when they arrived in Britain.
   b. Why do you think so many British people were so keen to blame the Irish for their problems?

Causation

Explain why Irish migration to Britain increased during the eighteenth and nineteenth centuries.

You may use the following in your answer:
- industrial revolution
- famine

You must also use information of your own.

Migration Nation

2.3 Irish people in modern Britain

There was a large increase in Irish immigration in the 1800s. There were two main reasons for this. Firstly, many came to escape extreme poverty in parts of Ireland, and to find better paid work during the industrial revolution. Secondly, after 1846, over one and a half million Irish people came to Britain to escape famine during the Great Hunger. These migrants often faced great difficulties when they got to Britain, but despite this, into the twentieth century and beyond many continued to migrate. Why did Irish people migrate in more modern times? Why did Irish migrants settle in particular places? And what was the impact of Irish migration on Britain?

Objectives

- Explain why Irish people migrated to Britain in modern times.
- Examine the impact of Irish migration.

Migration in the twentieth century

For many years, large numbers of Irish people migrated to the USA. At some points in US history, there were more Irish people migrating to the USA than people from any other nation. However, in the 1920s, the US government began to limit the number of migrants coming into the country. As a result of these restrictions, Britain instead became the main destination for the hundreds of thousands of Irish people who wanted a new life abroad. This meant that, by the 1930s, approximately four out of every five migrants who left Ireland migrated to Britain. There were no restrictions on Irish migration to Britain before 1939, but special permits were required during (and just after) the Second World War. No permits were required from 1952. Irish people continued to migrate in large numbers over the next few decades. The 1950s saw the peak in Irish migration, when between 50,000 and 60,000 people arrived in Britain from Ireland each year. By the early 1970s, around one million Irish-born people lived in Britain. In addition, many people from Northern Ireland migrated to Britain during the Troubles – a period of violent conflict in Northern Ireland between different groups that lasted from the late 1960s to 1998.

Where did Irish people settle?

Irish migrants settled where jobs were available, particularly in expanding towns and cities such as London, Liverpool, Manchester, Birmingham, Coventry, Glasgow and Luton. In Birmingham after the war, for example, there was a shortage of workers in car and textile factories, on building sites, in hospitals, and on buses and trains. Many of these jobs were filled by Irish migrants. In fact, an article published in 1952 stated that around one third of the workers on Birmingham's transport system were Irish women. In Luton, thousands of Irish migrants found work at the Vauxhall car factory and at Luton Airport.

▼ **SOURCE A** Adapted from an interview with a 36-year-old male Irish migrant, featured in the *Birmingham Gazette*, September 1951. He got a job in the Dunlop tyre factory on the day he arrived in Britain. In many towns and cities, particular areas became known for their large Irish populations – Digbeth and Sparkhill in Birmingham, East End Park in Leeds, and Kilburn and Camden Town in London.

'I was doing casual labouring in Dublin, Ireland, but even that ran out. I just couldn't get a job of any sort. I just couldn't keep a family of eight on the money I was getting. Now in England, I'm averaging £10 a week, and I never earned so much in my life.'

Irish heritage?

Today, there are large Irish communities in many British towns and cities, including Birmingham, London and Manchester. In 2001, a survey by the Irish brewer Guinness found that one in four people living in Britain claimed to have an Irish background. A 2010 survey revealed that over 70 per cent of Londoners claimed to have Irish ancestry. People with Irish roots have made an important, long-lasting contribution to British life. Indeed, Irish bars, clubs and traditions have become part of British culture – and even football teams such as Aston Villa, Arsenal, Celtic, Everton and Manchester United have a tradition of representing the Irish communities in their area. There are many prominent Irish migrants, and their descendents. There are talented writers, artists and musicians.

▼ **SOURCE B** The Beatles are arguably the most influential pop group of all time. Formed in Liverpool by school friends John Lennon, Paul McCartney and George Harrison, they were later joined by drummer Ringo Starr. Three of the Beatles have Irish ancestry: John Lennon's great-grandparents were Irish migrants, Paul McCartney had an Irish grandfather and great-grandfather, and George Harrison's mother was from an Irish migrant family.

▼ **SOURCE C** St Patrick's Day is a cultural and religious celebration held on 17 March each year, the traditional date of the death of St Patrick, the main patron saint of Ireland. St Patrick's Day parades, such as this one in Birmingham, are often held in cities where there is a large Irish community.

▼ **SOURCE D** Ant & Dec (Anthony McPartlin and Declan Donnelly) are a popular British television presenting duo with strong Irish roots. Dec, for example, is the child of Irish parents, who moved to Newcastle upon Tyne in the 1950s.

Fact

Liverpool is known for having perhaps the strongest Irish connections of any UK city. In fact, around three quarters of Liverpudlians claim to be of Irish descent. This originates from Liverpool being one of the closest major ports to Ireland, which made it easier for migrants to travel there. Also, some language experts think that the famous Liverpudlian ('Scouse') accent has been heavily influenced by migration and is a hybrid of Irish and Welsh accents combining with the traditional Lancashire accent.

Fact

Many Irish nurses already worked in British hospitals but, when the National Health Service was created in 1948, more migrated to Britain. It has been estimated that, by 1971, 12 per cent of Britain's nurses were from Ireland.

Over to You

1. a Where in Britain did many Irish migrants settle in the twentieth century?
   b Suggest reasons why they settled in these places.
2. Why did Britain, rather than the USA, become the main destination for Irish migrants by the 1930s?

Source Analysis

Study **Source A**. How useful is this source to a historian studying Irish migration in the twentieth century?

Later on... TODAY

Of all the migrants who entered the USA between 1851 and 1860, it is estimated that 81 per cent (around 990,000) were Irish. Today, over 40 million US citizens (about one sixth of the population) identify their national background as Irish.

2 Have you been learning?

Quick Knowledge Quiz

Choose the correct answer from the three options:

1. In the 1840s, a disease destroyed the Irish potato crop. What was it called?
   a. black spot
   b. potato blight
   c. potato mould

2. The failure of the potato crop caused a terrible famine known as the Great Hunger. How many people died?
   a. around 500,000 (one sixteenth of the population)
   b. around one million (one eighth of the population)
   c. around four million (half of the population)

3. Irish migration increased during the years of the Great Hunger. How many Irish-born people were living in the UK by the 1860s?
   a. 25,000
   b. 100,000
   c. 600,000

4. What is a navvy?
   a. an Irish migrant worker
   b. an Irish person
   c. a worker who built canals, railways and roads

5. In the 1920s, Britain became the main destination for Irish people wishing to migrate abroad. Why?
   a. because the British government invited Irish people to migrate
   b. because the USA introduced restrictions on migration
   c. because restrictions on migration to the UK were ended

6. Which of the following were built mainly by Irish migrant workers?
   a. the Houses of Parliament and Big Ben
   b. the railways and the Royal Albert Dock
   c. the Tower of London and Windsor Castle

7. What religion were most Irish migrants?
   a. Catholic
   b. Protestant
   c. Jewish

8. Many Irish migrants found jobs in the NHS. In 1971, what proportion of NHS nurses were Irish?
   a. 1 per cent
   b. 12 per cent
   c. 50 per cent

9. According to a 2001 survey, what proportion of people in Britain claim to have Irish heritage?
   a. one in ten
   b. one in eight
   c. one in four

10. St Patrick's Day is a cultural and religious celebration. Cities with a large Irish community often hold parades. When is St Patrick's Day?
    a. 15 February
    b. 17 March
    c. 19 April

Chapter 2: Irish migration

Have you been learning?

Writing in detail

Look at the paragraph below. It is a very basic answer to this question:

What was the Great Hunger and why did it begin?

However, the answer does not contain many specific, factual details. Rewrite the paragraph to include more detail – adding names, dates, examples and facts where possible. It might be a good idea to re-read pages 32–33 before you start.

> The Great Hunger was a time when lots of people starved because there was a problem with the potato harvest.

- When did this happen? And where? Be specific.
- Perhaps add figures. Details will improve answers.
- What was the problem? Mention 'potato blight' here. Also, you could point out that potatoes were a main source of food. You might even mention the poverty of the Irish peasants at this point.
- How about going a stage further? You might 'show off' your knowledge by writing how the British government (that controlled Ireland) did little to help the starving Irish people – which might have made the disaster worse.

Note-taking

Note-taking is a vital skill. To do it successfully, you must pick out all the important (key) words in a sentence. The important words are those that are vital to the meaning (and your understanding) of the sentence. For example, in the sentences:

> Irish migrants got jobs in a number of different industries, including working in mines and in cotton mills. They contributed to the expansion of Britain's towns and cities and its overall industrial growth. Many Irish migrants found jobs all around the country as navvies, building canals, roads, railways and docks. In 1850, around a quarter of a million navvies were employed on the railways, and one third of these were Irish.

… the important words and phrases are:

Irish migrants; jobs; mines/cotton mills in expanding towns/cities; navvies built canals/roads/railways/docks; 1850 = 250,000 navvies worked on railways and 1/3 Irish.

The original sentences totalled over 65 words, but the shortened version is around 25 words long and contains abbreviations.

Note-taking like this will help your understanding of events – and will provide you with a great revision exercise.

1. Write down the important words in the following sentences. These important words are your notes.

   a. Building railways was hard, dangerous work that involved using gunpowder, picks and shovels to clear the way for the railway line. Navvies had a reputation for being strong and hard-working. Between 1839 and 1852, navvies built the Woodhead Tunnel under the Pennines between Sheffield and Manchester. The work was so dangerous that the navvies who built it suffered a higher death rate than the soldiers who fought at the Battle of Waterloo.

   b. In the early years, navvies had to travel with the railways as they were built, so they lived in makeshift huts next to the bridges, tunnels and cuttings they were building. They developed their own lifestyle and culture and gained a reputation for heavy drinking and fighting.

   c. By 1861, there were around 600,000 Irish-born people in Britain. Like many migrant groups, before or since, the Irish tended to live close together in towns and cities. Despite getting work, they were not wealthy, and often ended up in the poorest quality housing in the worst parts of town.

   d. Britain was not the only destination for Irish migrants – nearly one million travelled to the USA. Today, large communities with Irish ancestry can be found in many US cities including Philadelphia, Chicago and Boston.

Big Question 5: Why did Black people migrate to Britain before the twentieth century?

Until recently, less attention has been given to Black people living in Britain before the twentieth century, even though there has been a Black presence in Britain for hundreds of years. However, dedicated historians have begun to look into the long history of the Black presence in Britain. So, who were the earliest Black Britons? What brought them here? And what do we know about their lives?

Objectives

- Examine the history of the presence of people of African origin in Britain.
- Investigate the life of John Blanke.

Roman Africans in Britain

Africans have been living in Britain since at least Roman times. For example, by the third century CE, several Roman officers and soldiers had come to Britain from the continent of Africa. There is strong evidence that a unit of 500 African soldiers guarded a fort on Hadrian's Wall, which marked the edge of the Roman Empire in Britain. In 193CE, Septimius Severus became Rome's first African emperor (see **Source A**). He lived in Britain for three years before his death in York in 211CE.

▼ **SOURCE A** A painting from Egypt, around 200CE, of Emperor Septimius Severus and his wife, Empress Julia Domna. Severus is well known for the way he treated his soldiers. He improved wages and allowed them to marry, for example. His treatment of the soldiers was copied by future emperors.

Later on... 1901

Recent analysis of a female skeleton found in York in 1901 (now on display in the Yorkshire Museum) revealed that although the woman was probably born and raised in Roman Britain, she was most likely to be of North African descent. She was buried with beautiful bracelets, bangles, beads and glass, indicating that she was very wealthy. She is now commonly known as the 'Ivory Bangle Lady'.

▼ **INTERPRETATION B** Scientists have reconstructed how the 'Ivory Bangle Lady' might have looked when she was alive.

Into the Middle Ages

There are records of people of African descent living in England in the Middle Ages too. For example, in the 1200s, a medieval monk wrote that London contained 'every race of men, out of every nation', including 'Garamantes' – a word used at the time to describe people from northern Africa. In 1993, a skeleton of an African man (nicknamed the 'Ipswich Man') was found in the cemetery of a monastery in Ipswich; he had been buried around 1250.

Black Tudors and Stuarts

During the era of the Tudors (1485–1603) and the Stuarts (1603–1714), Black people could be found living across England, in cities such as London, Plymouth, Bristol and Southampton, as well as in more rural places such as Worcestershire and Devon. The parish records from St Botolph without Aldgate (in the East End of London) show how multicultural some areas of the country were in Tudor times. In this area in the late 1500s, there were French and Dutch people, some people from India, one person from Persia (modern-day Iran), and 25 people of African origin. Most were employed as servants, but not all. Black Tudors also worked as weavers, labourers, sailors and musicians.

Legal status

The Black people living in Britain at this time were not enslaved. Although Britain participated in the slave trade abroad, it was illegal to enslave people within the British Isles. They were paid wages, and were able to earn their own living, testify in court, and be baptised and married by the Church. At the time of Elizabeth I, for example, some historians think that as many as a thousand Black people lived in England. They lived and worked at many levels of society – from royal households to more 'ordinary' jobs such as servants, weavers and entertainers.

Fact

Historians have discovered lots of fascinating information about other Black Tudors. For example, Jacques Francis was an expert diver who salvaged guns from the wreck of the ship *Mary Rose*. He was the first known African to give evidence in an English court.

Big Question

INTERPRETATION C From an article written by historian Dr Onyeka Nubia, who works at the University of Nottingham and Edgehill University.

'Some [...] Africans and their descendants were born in Tudor England and others had origins from the Iberian Peninsula [Spain and Portugal]. Africans also came to England from kingdoms in West and North Africa and some people arrived via the Caribbean and Central America. These last sets of peoples were often connected to English merchant adventurers.

It is not possible to know the exact number of Africans living in early modern England. But they were certainly more than a few isolated individuals.'

Fact

It was not uncommon to find African sailors working on English ships. Diego, an enslaved African man, helped Sir Francis Drake fight the Spanish in Panama. In doing so, Diego was able to escape from enslavement. He returned to England with Drake and joined him in his attempt to circumnavigate the globe from 1577 to 1580. John Anthony, an African man, was taken from a Spanish ship by an English pirate called John Mainwaring around 1613. Anthony also became a pirate, then eventually settled in Dover, Kent and worked as a sailor. In 1718, Blackbeard's ship had a crew of 100, 60 of whom were Black.

Over to You

1. Read **Interpretation C**. In your own words explain what Dr Nubia is saying about England's Black population in Tudor times.
2. Look at **Source A**.
   a. Who was Septimius Severus?
   b. How useful is this source to a historian studying the history of Africans living in Britain?

Why did Black people migrate to Britain before the twentieth century?

John Blanke: the royal musician

Look at **Source D**. It is part of a 20-metre-long painted vellum scroll, known as the Westminster Tournament Roll. It was made to commemorate a grand jousting tournament held in London to celebrate the birth of one of King Henry VIII's children. The king and queen appear several times, surrounded by servants, nobles, soldiers and entertainers – including six musicians on horseback playing trumpets. One of the trumpeters is a Black musician called John Blanke, and he is the only identifiable Black person to have been shown in sixteenth-century English art.

What happened to John Blanke?

There are no records of John Blanke in England after 1512. Some historians think he moved to France, or another European country, to find work. A French tapestry showing a famous meeting in 1520 between King Henry VIII and King Francis I of France includes a Black trumpeter. The banner on his trumpet shows the emblem of France. Could this be John Blanke? Other historians have suggested that Blanke may have died in battle (trumpeters sometimes directed soldiers during battles), or in a fire in the Palace of Westminster in 1512.

John Blanke: what historians know

- Unknown origins: John Blanke was probably not his birth name. His surname may have started out as a nickname.
- 1501: Blanke arrives in England, probably from Spain with Catherine of Aragon when she comes to marry Arthur (the eldest son of King Henry VII).
- 1502: Blanke appears in the record for the first time among the trumpeters playing at Prince Arthur's funeral at Worcester Cathedral in April.
- 1507: Henry VII's first known payment of wages to 'John Blanke, the blacke Trumpet' in early December 1507 shows he is paid 20 shillings a month. Monthly payments for the same amount continue throughout the following year.
- 1509: In May, Blanke (dressed in black) plays at the funeral of Henry VII; in June, he plays at the coronation of Henry VIII (this time in scarlet clothing).
- 1509: Blanke writes to King Henry VIII to ask for a pay rise – and gets it! He complains that his current wage is 'not sufficient to maintain and keep him' and reminds the king of the 'true and faithful service' he performs daily and intends to continue for the rest of his life.
- 1511: Blanke performs at the Westminster Tournament over two days in February.
- 1512: Blanke gets married. We don't know who he marries, but there is a record that Henry VIII orders a new wedding outfit for him 'to be taken of our gift against his marriage'. The gift is a gown of violet cloth, a bonnet and a hat.
- 1514: A full list of the king's trumpeters is drawn up in January. Blanke's name isn't on the list. The king's wedding present in 1512 is the last surviving reference to John Blanke.

◀ **SOURCE D** Part of the Westminster Tournament Roll from 1511. John Blanke appears twice on the scroll. He wears a turban each time, which is brown and yellow in the first appearance, and green and gold in the second (pictured here).

The trade in enslaved Africans

Towards the end of Tudor times, and for the next few hundred years, Britain became heavily involved in what was known as the 'slave trade'. As a consequence, many Black Africans were brought to Britain by people involved in the trade. Some of the Black Africans had been made free by their enslavers, but their legal position was unclear. Others were treated as property by the people who brought them to Britain, but they were considered free and could not be forced to return to their enslavers if they escaped. However, if they were kidnapped back to the Caribbean, they would be enslaved again.

▼ **INTERPRETATION E** From *Black Tudors: The Untold Story* by historian Miranda Kaufmann. In this book, Kaufmann pieces together evidence about the lives of ten Black men and women living in Britain in Tudor times. Here she explains why studying the lives of Black Tudors is important.

> 'These ten men and women are but a small fraction of the hundreds of Africans who lived in […] England. Many are recorded by no more than a one-line entry in a parish record or tax return […] But as increasing numbers of records become digitised […] and electronically searchable, the task should become more manageable. And if what has already been found is anything to go by, it will prove worthwhile. Why? Because anyone who assumed that all Africans in British History have been powerless, enslaved victims must be challenged. The Black Tudors actively pursued their own interests and were free to do so. We find them petitioning [asking] for the payment of wages or for a pay rise, guarding trade secrets, […] seeking baptism as a path to social acceptance. More often than not their efforts were rewarded […] It is vital to understand that the British Isles have always been peopled with immigrants. The Black Tudors are just one of a series of different peoples who arrived on these shores in centuries past.'

Big Question

▼ **SOURCE F** A painting entitled *Captain Graham in his cabin* by William Hogarth. Black servants and entertainers appear in many paintings in the 1600s and 1700s.

Over to You

1. Look at **Source D**.
   a. What can you infer from the source about John Blanke's status in Tudor times?
   b. Why is this image so important?
2. Why are historians unsure about Blanke's life after 1512?
3. Write a 200-word entry on John Blanke's life for the *Children's Dictionary of National Biography*. You should include facts about his life and consider why our understanding of his life is important.

Knowledge and Understanding

Complete the sentences below with an accurate word or words.
- The earliest Black Britons we know of lived during the time of …
- Black Britons in Tudor times worked in a number of different jobs including …
- Historians think John Blanke arrived in England from …
- There is a record of John Blanke writing to Henry VIII asking for …

Migration Nation   43

3.1 Caribbean migration before the Second World War

In the first few years following the Second World War (1939–1945), a number of passenger ships began arriving in Britain carrying migrants from the Caribbean. The most famous ship to have arrived was called the *Empire Windrush*, which docked in London on 22 June 1948. There were 1,027 passengers on board, including hundreds of people from the Caribbean. Many people today regard this as the beginning of migration to Britain from this region – but it wasn't. There is a long history of migration from the Caribbean, dating back hundreds of years. Many of those people were of African descent. This chapter explores the link between people of African descent and lots of the islands in the Caribbean, such as Jamaica, Barbados, Bermuda, and Trinidad and Tobago. It will examine the reasons why people from the Caribbean migrated to Britain and what their experiences were like when they arrived.

Objectives

- Examine the presence of African-Caribbean people in Britain up to the Second World War.
- Explore the stories of some African-Caribbean Britons.

The trade in enslaved Africans

By the mid-1600s, Britain was heavily involved in what was known as the 'slave trade'. West African men, women and children were captured, sold and taken by force across the Atlantic Ocean to North and South America, and Caribbean islands such as Jamaica, Barbados, Bermuda, and Trinidad and Tobago. Here, they were forced to work on large farms (called plantations) all their lives, without wages, and in great hardship. It is estimated that Britain transported 3.1 million Africans to British colonies in North and South America and Caribbean islands between 1562 and 1807. Conditions were so bad on the ships that only 2.7 million of these enslaved people survived the journey.

The trade made Britain a very wealthy country. It provided slave owners with unpaid workers who farmed expensive goods such as sugar, cotton and tobacco, which were sold for huge profits. These profits helped fund Britain's industrial revolution, which made the country even richer.

From the Caribbean to Britain

The link between people of African descent, the Caribbean and Britain mostly begins at the time of this trade. Many plantation owners and slave traders from the Caribbean islands brought enslaved people back to Britain when they returned home. Some of these people had been made free by their enslavers, but their legal position was unclear.

African-Caribbean people in Britain

In 1807, the British Parliament passed a law that made it illegal to transport enslaved Africans to the British Empire in order to sell them. However, enslaved people who were already in the colonies were not made free, and could still be bought and sold by local slave owners. In 1833, Parliament banned slave ownership too.

We do not know how many African-Caribbean people were living in Britain by this time. However, we know that most worked as servants or labourers and lived in overcrowded housing in the industrial towns, cities and ports. Some found themselves living on the streets and begging. Black people faced lots of discrimination and were not always welcomed, and found it difficult to get work as a result. However, despite facing many challenges, some African-Caribbean people were very successful.

Mary Prince

Mary Prince was born in Bermuda around 1787 into an enslaved family of African descent. She was bought and sold several times in her early life. In 1828, Prince arrived in London with a family who had enslaved her, and managed to escape from their house. In 1831, Prince's story was published – the first published account of enslavement from a Black woman's perspective. Source A appears in the final chapter of her story.

▼ **SOURCE A** From *The History of Mary Prince, related by herself*, 1831.

'All slaves want to be free - to be free is very sweet. I will say the truth to English people who may read this history [...] I have been a slave myself - I know what slaves feel - I can tell by myself what other slaves feel, and by what they have told me. The man that says slaves be quite happy in slavery - that they don't want to be free - that man is either ignorant or a lying person.'

Mary Seacole

Born in 1805 on the Caribbean island of Jamaica, Seacole's father was a Scottish soldier (working on the island) and her mother was a Jamaican nurse and healer of African descent. Seacole travelled to London in the early 1850s and later used her own money to travel to Crimea (in Eastern Europe) to help British soldiers fighting in a war there. She showed great determination and courage and earned the respect of the soldiers. After the war, Seacole returned to England, but she was ill and bankrupt. However, people raised money for her in gratitude for her work in the war. She also wrote a book, which became a best seller.

▶ **SOURCE B** A memorial to Mary Seacole in the grounds of St Thomas' Hospital, London.

Key Words Caribbean

Walter Tull

Born in Folkestone in 1888, Tull was the son of a carpenter who had migrated from Barbados. Tull's grandfather had been an enslaved person there, but was freed. In 1909, Tull became one of Britain's first Black professional footballers, playing for Tottenham Hotspur and Northampton Town. During the First World War he was in the Footballers' Battalion of the Middlesex Regiment and fought in the Battle of the Somme in 1916. He was the first Black officer in the British Army to command white soldiers. He was killed in action in March 1918, aged 29.

▶ **SOURCE C** The Tottenham Hotspur Football Club team photograph of the 1911–1912 season. Walter Tull is pictured on the third row down.

William Cuffay

William Cuffay was born on a ship in 1788 and was the son of a former enslaved man from St Kitts in the Caribbean. His family later settled in Kent and he worked as a tailor. He became a leading figure in the campaign to improve voting rights in Britain. At the time, only property-owning men could vote. Cuffay believed that everyone should have a vote. He was transported to Australia as a punishment in 1848 for allegedly planning an uprising against the British government. After he completed his sentence, he remained there.

Over to You

1. Describe some reasons why African-Caribbean people arrived in Britain in the eighteenth and nineteenth centuries. Give examples.

2. List some jobs that African-Caribbean migrants did after slavery was abolished.

3. Mary Prince, Mary Seacole, Walter Tull and William Cuffay regularly appear on lists of 'Great Black Britons'.
   a. Write a brief 25-word paragraph for each of them.
   b. Why do you think they each appear on the list?

3.2A The Windrush generation

On 22 June 1948, a ship named the *Empire Windrush* landed at Tilbury Docks near London. On board were 1,027 passengers – including several hundred from the Caribbean – who had come to live in Britain. This was an event that would change British society forever. So, why did they move to Britain? How were they treated? And how did they help change life in Britain?

Objectives

- Define the term 'Windrush generation'.
- Outline the experiences and impacts of the Windrush generation.

Migrating to Britain

Many people from Britain's Caribbean **colonies** had contributed to Britain's effort in the Second World War. When the fighting ended, some stayed in Britain, but most went back home. But life was very hard in the Caribbean and poverty and hardship were common. However, many had been taught in school that Britain was the 'mother country' where they would always feel supported and welcome. As a result, many ambitious young Caribbean people decided that they would migrate to Britain in search of new opportunities.

▼ **SOURCE A**

The *Empire Windrush* arriving at Tilbury Docks, near London, on 22 June 1948. The Caribbean migrants who arrived in Britain became known as the 'Windrush generation'.

46 Chapter 3: Caribbean migration

Why Britain?

Britain was very short of workers after the war. In part, this was because many British people had migrated to countries such as Canada and Australia, in search of a better life. In Britain, large areas of many cities had been destroyed by enemy bombing. A programme of rebuilding began, which needed workers. Also, the newly created National Health Service (NHS) and an improving transport system needed workers too.

In July 1948, the British Nationality Act was passed. It clarifies the right of people living in countries throughout the British **Empire** – now known as the 'Commonwealth' – to live permanently and work in Britain. Many people in the Empire and Commonwealth had been brought up speaking English and knew all about Britain from their lessons in school. Many had been to Britain as members of the armed forces during the war. The NHS, London Transport, the British Hotels and Restaurants Association and the British Transport Commission all encouraged people from the Caribbean to move to Britain.

▼ **SOURCE B** Adapted from an article in *The Guardian* newspaper on 23 June 1948. The term 'coloured' was used at the time to describe Black people, but it is considered offensive today.

'What manner of men are these *Empire Windrush* has brought to Britain? This morning, on the decks, I spoke with the following: an apprentice accountant, a farm worker, a tailor, a boxer, a mechanic, a singer, and a law student. Or thus they described themselves.
And what had made them leave Jamaica? In most cases, lack of work. Most of the married men have left their wives and children at home, and hope to send for them later.
They are, then, as mixed a collection of humanity as one might find. Some will be good workers, some bad. No doubt the singers will find audiences somewhere. But the more worldly-wise among them are conscious of the deeper problem posed. In the past Britain has welcomed displaced persons who cannot go home.
"This is right," said one of the immigrants. "Surely then, there is nothing against our coming, for we are British subjects. If there is – is it because we are coloured?"'

Key Words   colony   empire

Welcome, *Empire Windrush*?

The ship's voyage made headlines in Britain before it had even docked, even though the *Empire Windrush* wasn't the first ship to bring Caribbean migrants to Britain in this period. Although many migrants from Europe had been entering Britain since the war, and a small part of the population was already made up of Black Britons, the arrival of this ship caused alarm. Newspapers were full of stories of the 'colour problem' heading towards Britain's shores and some MPs demanded that the ship should be turned around.

> **Fact**
>
> 'Coloured' and 'Black' were terms used to describe African, Caribbean and Asian people until the late twentieth century. 'Coloured' is not a term commonly used anymore because it is offensive.

> **Over to You**
>
> 1 What was the British Nationality Act?
>
> 2 List reasons why people from the Caribbean may have chosen to come to Britain after the Second World War.
>
> 3 Read **Source B**.
>   a List at least five different jobs that the passengers on the ship claimed they could do.
>   b Why, according to the article, have the passengers left their homes in the Caribbean?
>   c According to the writer of the article, which passengers on board will definitely find work?
>   d According to one of the passengers interviewed, why might some of the existing population of Britain be against their arrival?

3.2B The Windrush generation

The British experience

It wasn't long before the passengers on the *Empire Windrush* found jobs in Britain. Many more migrants from the Caribbean followed in search of work. By 1961, there were 161,000 Caribbean-born people living in Britain. Like the original Windrush migrants, the new arrivals settled in industrial cities, such as Liverpool, Manchester, Birmingham and Nottingham. Most, however, stayed in London. They came with a variety of skills – some were electricians, mechanics and engineers, for example. Some found good jobs but many, regardless of their qualifications (which often weren't recognised in Britain), ended up working in low-paid jobs such as cleaners, ticket collectors and hospital porters. They also experienced difficulties finding decent places to live, and tensions between migrants and existing populations began to grow. Thousands of white migrants also settled in Britain after the Second World War. However, hostility was more often than not reserved for Black migrants. Racism was present in every aspect of their new lives in Britain.

▼ **INTERPRETATION D** A Caribbean nurse recalls her early experiences of living and working in Britain.

'When I first started coming in the country and was nursing, the older patient was not used to Black people so they were very nasty. [...] Black people, we were treated differently [...] but we didn't worry because we know what we wanted to achieve and what we had to do and we did it, and we did it by making jokes with each other and laughing and doing our work properly.'

▼ **INTERPRETATION E** Sam King, a passenger on the *Empire Windrush*, interviewed by the BBC in 1998. King had served in Britain in the Royal Air Force during the war, but went home in 1947. He returned on the *Empire Windrush* and went on to become the first Black mayor of Southwark, London.

'The second day in England I was offered five jobs. If someone want to leave, let them leave, but I have been here during the war fighting Nazi Germany and I came back and help build Britain. People said that we would not stay longer than one year; we are here, and I and my people are here to stay.'

Earlier on... 1915

In 1915, during the First World War, volunteers from the Caribbean were accepted into the British Army. A new regiment called the British West Indies Regiment was formed. Many African-Caribbean people served in the Merchant Navy too. The Merchant Navy was the collective name for the ships that transported food and raw materials. After the war, many of these men came to live in Britain. They often settled in port cities and towns like Liverpool, London and Newport.

◀ **SOURCE C** Many of the new arrivals settled in large industrial cities such as London or Birmingham. They faced prejudice and difficulty finding housing, as shown in the racist sign below. At this time, people of both African and Asian descent were often referred to as 'black'.

Earlier on...
1930

In 1930, a German passenger ship named *Monte Rosa* was launched. During the Second World War she was used as a troopship. In 1942 and 1943 she was used to deport Jewish people from Norway and Denmark. At the end of the war she was taken by the British and renamed – the *Empire Windrush*.

▼ **SOURCE F** In 1964, Daphne Steele, who was born in Guyana, became the first Black matron in a British hospital. Many other migrants from the Windrush generation worked in the NHS.

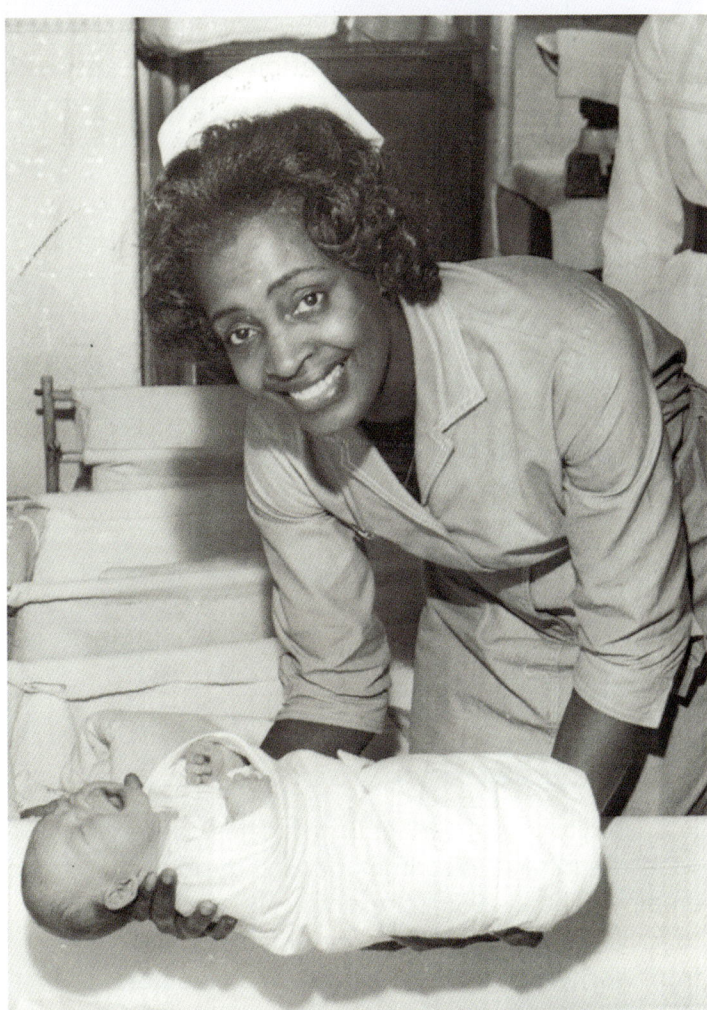

Key Words racism

Meanwhile...
1947–1948

The 1,027 passengers on the *Empire Windrush* came from a variety of places including Guyana, Jamaica, Trinidad, and Bermuda, among others. There were also 66 Polish refugees on board the *Empire Windrush* when it arrived in Britain in 1948. They had found their way to Mexico during the Second World War, and were now planning a new life in Britain.

The *Empire Windrush* was one of the first ships carrying migrants from the Caribbean – but it was not the first. In the spring of 1947, *Ormonde* landed at Liverpool Docks, and in December 1947, *Almanzora* landed at Southampton Docks, carrying passengers from the Caribbean.

Over to You

1 a What was the *Empire Windrush*?
   b Who were the 'Windrush generation'?

2 What barriers did African-Caribbean people face when they arrived in Britain?

3 Look at **Source C** and **Interpretation E**.
   a What does **Source C** show?
   b Summarise the experience of Sam King.
   c How useful are **Source C** and **Interpretation E** for an enquiry into the experiences of African-Caribbean migrants after the Second World War?

Causation

Explain why many people wanted to leave the Caribbean at the end of the Second World War.

Migration Nation **49**

3.3A The Caribbean experience in the 1950s, 1960s and 1970s

Between 1948 and 1952, 1,000–2,000 people moved to Britain from the Caribbean each year. The numbers rose rapidly in the years that followed and, in 1957, just over 40,000 migrants arrived. Official figures show that by 1961 there were just over 161,000 people who had been born in the Caribbean living in England and Wales: 90,000 men and just over 71,000 women. Migrants from the Caribbean outnumbered all other migrants from all other areas of the world. At this time, tension began to grow between the migrants and the existing populations in big cities, such as London, Birmingham and Liverpool. What were the key triggers of this tension? Where did tension turn to violence? How did the authorities and the migrant communities react?

Objectives

- Describe the experience of Caribbean people in Britain in the 1950s, 1960s and 1970s.
- Explore how Caribbean people fought for equal rights.
- Examine ways in which British governments responded to the growing tension between the existing population and migrants.

Tension grows

The existing populations of towns and cities with large migrant communities felt that migrant workers were making their lives harder, taking their jobs, and competing with them for limited housing. Some of the existing populations wanted an end to all migration into Britain, and wanted migrants to return to the countries they were born in. In many places, an unofficial **'colour bar'** was introduced. This was a racist system that meant that Black and Asian people were denied the opportunities that were available to white people. They were limited in the jobs they could get, the houses they could live in, and the restaurants and cafes they could enter. In late August 1958, tension reached boiling point and a series of violent attacks were launched against members of the Caribbean community in Nottingham and in Notting Hill, London.

Fact ✓

In response to racial discrimination, British Civil Rights movements developed as migrant communities fought back against the treatment they were experiencing. Groups such as the Universal Coloured People's Association, the Black Liberation Front, and the Black Panthers campaigned for better living and working conditions in Black communities.

▶ **SOURCE A** The 'colour bar' in action in the 1960s. Here, a worker of African-Caribbean descent sees that the jobs at this factory are not open to him. Note that the word 'coloured' is now considered offensive.

The Bristol Bus Boycott

In Bristol, as in many other British cities, there was widespread racial discrimination in housing and employment. In 1955, for example, bus workers agreed to a rule that banned Black and Asian men and women from working on buses as drivers or conductors. The bus company's leaders went along with the decision its workers had made and, by the early 1960s, no Black or Asian man or woman had ever been hired to work on Bristol's buses.

In 1961, a local newspaper, the *Bristol Evening Post*, published a series of articles on the racist employment practices at the bus company. Soon, a campaign group emerged, founded by a core of local African-Caribbean migrants: Owen Henry, Roy Hackett, Audley Evans and Prince Brown. Known as the West Indian Development Council, they were later joined by Paul Stephenson as spokesperson. Stephenson was a political activist with a West African father and an English mother of mixed ancestry.

Stephenson, inspired by the work of Martin Luther King Jr, Rosa Parks, and other non-violent civil rights activists in the USA, hatched a plan to expose the racist policies of the bus company. Over the telephone, he managed to get a young man named Guy Bailey an interview for a job as a bus conductor in April 1963. However, when Bailey arrived and the bus company realised he was a Black Jamaican, he was told he could no longer be interviewed (see **Interpretation C**).

In response, Stephenson announced a **boycott** of Bristol's buses. He said that none of the city's Caribbean community would use the buses. Some students (and tutors) from Bristol University staged a protest march in the city centre in support. Some local residents joined them. They were shouted at by angry bus workers.

The Bristol Bus Boycott soon became national and international news. Prime Minister Harold Wilson, local politician Tony Benn, and famous West Indies cricketer and diplomat Sir Learie Constantine all supported the boycott. Eventually, with pressure growing on the bus company, it announced that it would end its 'colour bar'. The announcement was made on 28 August 1963, the same day that Martin Luther King Jr made his famous 'I Have a Dream' speech in Washington. In September, a Sikh named Raghbir Singh became Bristol's first non-white bus conductor. Soon after, he was joined by Norman Samuels and Norris Edwards from Jamaica, and Mohammed Raschid and Abbas Ali from Pakistan.

▼ **SOURCE B** A mural celebrating Roy Hackett and the Bristol Bus Boycott, which can be seen on the end wall of a row of terraced houses in St Paul's in Bristol. It was painted in 2018/2019 but collapsed in 2021. There are, however, plans to reinstate it.

Key Words
'colour bar'   boycott

▼ **INTERPRETATION C** Guy Bailey, who was born in Jamaica, moved to Britain as a young man. In a book published in 2019, he recalls his attempt to get a job as a bus conductor in 1963, and the racism he experienced.

'I did apply for a job as a bus conductor and an interview was arranged for me to come to the bus station for an interview [...] when I actually got to the reception area, the receptionist said to the manager, "Oh, Mr Bailey is here; he's Black." And the manager then spoke with me and explained that he wasn't prepared to offer me an interview because if I did he would "displease his bus crew".'

Fact
Some other cities, such as London, Wolverhampton and Manchester, did employ Black and Asian bus drivers and conductors.

Over to You

1. **a** What is a 'colour bar'?
   b Give two examples of a 'colour bar' in Britain in the 1950s.

2. **a** Describe the events leading up to, and including, the Bristol Bus Boycott. Make sure you include names, dates, and who supported the boycott (and who didn't).
   b Suggest why there weren't similar boycotts in London, Wolverhampton and Manchester.

Source Analysis
How could you follow up **Source B** to find out more about the Bristol Bus Boycott?

In your answer, you must give the question you would ask and the type of source you could use.

Note down:
- detail in in **Source B** that I would follow up
- question I would ask
- what type of source I could use
- how this might help answer my question.

Migration Nation

3.3B The Caribbean experience in the 1950s, 1960s and 1970s

The governments' responses

Different British governments responded to the growing tension between the existing populations and migrants in two ways. Some tried to limit immigration. Some tried to tackle racial discrimination.

Act of Parliament	What it meant for migrant groups
Commonwealth Immigrants Act 1962	Commonwealth citizens who did not own a British passport could only enter Britain if they were skilled professionals who had been given permission to work in Britain.
Race Relations Act 1965	The first British law to directly address racism. It made discrimination illegal on the grounds of 'colour, race or ethnic or national origins'. This only applied in 'public places' such as hotels and pubs. It didn't cover housing, employment or financial matters such as mortgages and car insurance.
Commonwealth Immigrants Act 1968	Commonwealth immigrants were only allowed to live and work in Britain if they had a parent or grandparent who was born in Britain or was a British citizen.
Race Relations Act 1968	This made it illegal to refuse housing or employment to people because of their colour, race or national origins.

Fact ✓

The Times newspaper declared that Powell's speech was 'evil', but he also had many supporters. Some politicians argued that he had a right to voice his opinions, and 1,000 dockworkers in London went on strike in protest at his sacking. Groups supporting Powell's views, such as the National Front, became more popular too. Many members identified strongly with Hitler's policies in Nazi Germany. The National Front was known for using violence against minority ethnic groups, and would regularly intimidate and terrorise individuals.

Enoch Powell

In 1968, in Birmingham, a politician named Enoch Powell made a controversial (but very well known) speech about immigration. He said that white people were becoming 'strangers in their own country' and the government was allowing too many immigrants to settle in Britain, which was leading to overcrowding. He said that many 'decent, ordinary fellow Englishman' were worried that their wives might not be able to 'obtain hospital beds in childbirth' and that their children would not be able to 'obtain school places'. He predicted violent bloodshed if migrants were allowed to keep coming to Britain and were given equal rights with white people. Powell was sacked for making the speech – but surveys showed that around three-quarters of British people agreed with him.

▼ **SOURCE D** Porters from Smithfield meat market in London march to Westminster in support of Enoch Powell, 1968.

Chapter 3: Caribbean migration

SOURCE E A protest in Merthyr Tydfil, Wales, against a visit to Wales by Enoch Powell, 1971.

INTERPRETATION F Lance Bunkley, a young Jamaican migrant living in Wolverhampton in 1968, recalls his experiences in 2008 after Powell's speech.

'Before the speech, a lone Black man could walk home at night, but after that there was fear. I remember trying to help an elderly person on the bus and being told, "Take your Black hands off me."'

More laws

The government created more laws relating to immigration in the 1970s. The Immigration Act of 1971 severely restricted immigration from the Commonwealth, unless immigrants had a parent or grandparent born in Britain. However, in 1976, a new, tougher Race Relations Act was introduced. This Act outlawed all discrimination in employment, housing, education, provision of goods and services, and much more. The Act also set up the Commission for Racial Equality to make sure the new laws were followed.

Over to You

1. Why did some of the existing white populations resent British citizens from the Caribbean and other Commonwealth countries who arrived after 1945?

2. a How did British governments limit migration to Britain from Commonwealth countries in the 1960s?
   b Why do you think they introduced these limits?

3. Who was Enoch Powell, and why did he become so well known in 1968?

4. a Look at **Sources D and E** and **Interpretation F**. What can you learn from each about:
   - the impact of Enoch Powell's speech
   - race relations in the UK in the late 1960s?
   b What questions would you ask to find out more about these two things?

Fact
The number of immigrants (the number of people migrating *to* Britain) never exceeded the number of emigrants (the number of people migrating *from* Britain) throughout the 1950s, 1960s and most of the 1970s.

Knowledge and Understanding
Describe two ways British governments tried to improve the lives of migrants from the Caribbean and other Commonwealth countries.

3.4 The fight against prejudice

On 22 April 1993, a Black British student called Stephen Lawrence was waiting at a bus stop with a friend when a group of white teenagers launched an unprovoked, racist attack on him. Stephen was stabbed several times, and bled to death. He was 18 years old. During the police investigation that followed, many (including the Lawrence family) felt the police were not doing enough to identify and prosecute the killers because Stephen was Black. The murder of Stephen Lawrence led to a decades-long campaign against prejudice within the police force, and for his killers to be brought to justice.

Objectives

- Describe the events following the murder of Stephen Lawrence.
- Explore the consequences of the Windrush Scandal.

▶ **SOURCE A** Stephen Lawrence, taken shortly before his murder.

Institutional racism in the police

Charges against two suspects in the murder of Stephen Lawrence were dropped. The Lawrence family brought a private prosecution against the suspects, but that also failed. It looked as though nobody would be punished for Stephen's murder. However, after years of campaigning by Stephen's parents, the government set up a special inquiry into the police's handling of Stephen's murder. The outcome of the inquiry – known as the Macpherson report – concluded that the police investigation into Stephen's death had not been properly carried out because of 'professional incompetence, institutional racism and a failure of leadership'. It made over 70 recommendations that were designed to change the culture in the police force and other public bodies. These recommendations included targets for recruiting more officers from ethnic minorities, and setting up an Independent Police Complaints Commission to oversee the work of the police. Jack Straw, the government minister responsible for setting up the inquiry, said he wanted the report to 'act as a catalyst for permanent […] change, not just across our public services, but across the whole of society […] We must make equality a reality.'

Later on... 2012/2020

In 2012, two of the people originally suspected of killing Stephen Lawrence were found guilty of his murder. In 2020, the case was officially closed and it seems unlikely that the three remaining men involved will ever be brought to justice.

Fact ✓

The Macpherson report defined institutional racism as 'the collective failure of an organisation to provide […] [a] professional service […] through unwitting prejudice, ignorance, thoughtlessness and racist stereotyping which disadvantage minority ethnic people'.

Ongoing problems

The murder of Stephen Lawrence was an extreme example of racism. Britain's African-Caribbean communities continue to face a number of problems. For reasons that are still the subject of fierce controversy, exclusion rates for African-Caribbean students in English schools are up to six times higher than those of white students in some areas. Figures from 2021 also revealed that Black British drivers were 56 per cent more likely to be stopped by police than white British drivers.

Chapter 3: Caribbean migration

The Windrush Scandal

In 2012, the British government introduced new rules relating to migration. People now had to show documents proving they had a right to live in the country before they could rent a home, start a new job or receive medical treatment. This had devastating consequences for some of the Windrush generation. Many had arrived as children on their parents' passports and did not have their own documents. Others had been given permission to stay in the UK, but the government had not given them any documents, and had kept no records. In addition, many people who migrated from countries that were British colonies at the time believed that they were British citizens. Some of the people affected were sent back to the Caribbean. Others lost their jobs, or were stopped from having free medical care. This became known as the 'Windrush Scandal'. In August 2018, the British government admitted its mistakes and said that anyone who had left the UK would be helped to return.

▼ **SOURCE B** Demonstrators in London protesting at the government's treatment of the Windrush generation, 2018.

▼ **SOURCE C** From a 2018 interview with Tony Perry, who arrived in Britain in 1959 as a young child. He served in the Royal Navy and later became a social worker for a council in London. In 2001, he applied for a British passport and was refused after being told he wasn't a British citizen.

'I didn't want to tell anyone what happened; I felt ashamed […] It was like a punch in the stomach. I can't explain how it made me feel. I served on Her Majesty's behalf. I'm a British Jamaican West Indian Caribbean, but someone came and crossed a bit of that out; they erased a bit of my life […] I fell apart for about 10 years […] We were invited here, and then thrown away again, like so much rubbish […] This is a very dark chapter in British politics.'

Key Words   institutional racism

Meanwhile... 1996

Show Racism the Red Card is an anti-racism education charity. Footballer Shaka Hislop donated money to set up the charity in 1996, because he felt that education could effectively challenge the racist stereotypes and negative attitudes he had experienced. The charity uses football players to run educational workshops for young people and adults across Britain.

Earlier on... 1959

On 17 May 1959 in Notting Hill, London, a gang of white youths stabbed to death 32-year-old Kelso Cochrane, who was born on the Caribbean island of Antigua. The police failed to charge anyone for the murder. Family members are still campaigning for justice.

▶ A photo of Kelso Cochrane, taken a few months before he was murdered.

Over to You

1.
   a. Who was Stephen Lawrence?
   b. Why did it take so long to bring anyone to justice for his murder?

2.
   a. What was the Macpherson report?
   b. Define 'institutional racism'.
   c. Describe some of the recommendations of the Macpherson report.

3. Describe the Windrush Scandal in no more than 50 words.

Source Analysis

Read **Source C**.

How useful is **Source C** for a historian studying the Windrush Scandal?

Migration Nation

3.5 Activism and achievement

Source A shows a picture of Claudia Jones. She was born in Trinidad in the Caribbean and moved to Britain in 1955. In 1958, she set up Britain's first major Black weekly newspaper, the *West Indian Gazette And Afro-Asian Caribbean News*. Following the Notting Hill and Nottingham race riots in 1958, she helped to launch an annual carnival event in 1959, aimed at showing the culture and talent of the Caribbean to the people of Britain. She said she wanted to 'wash the taste of Notting Hill and Nottingham out of our mouths'. This event later became the Notting Hill Carnival, one of the largest street festivals in the world (see **Source B**). How have British Caribbean people shaped modern Britain?

Objectives
- Examine the role and legacy of Claudia Jones.
- Explore the experiences and achievements of British Caribbeans.

▶ **SOURCE A** Claudia Jones reading the *West Indian Gazette*, 1962. As well as setting up this newspaper, Jones campaigned against racist immigration policies and discrimination in housing, education and employment. She made speeches at peace rallies and visited Japan, Russia and China.

▼ **SOURCE B** The first outdoor Notting Hill carnival was held in 1966 and the event now attracts up to one million visitors from all backgrounds every year; this one was in 2012.

▼ **INTERPRETATION C** Corinne Skinner-Carter, speaking in 1996. Skinner-Carter was born in Trinidad and came to Britain in 1955 to train as a teacher. She later became an actress, starring in *EastEnders*.

'[Claudia] also started [...] a Black beauty contest. And this was before Black Power days. This was before we all knew that we were beautiful. We might not have known it but she knew that we were beautiful [...] And the first year there was a girl called Fay Craig that won this beauty contest, and I'm telling you, Fay Craig was Black, I mean really Black. But pretty. But without Claudia we would not have known that, because then we used to judge everybody's beauty by the European standard [...] The contests were a very popular feature of the carnival, attracting business sponsorship, as well as providing a career vehicle for some of the contestants.'

African-Caribbean impact

After the Second World War there was a shortage of workers in Britain. Caribbean migrants helped the British economy recover by filling jobs in hospitals, on railways, on building sites and on buses. Caribbean migrants were not the only new arrivals to Britain. They were joined by many from ex-British Empire countries such as Nigeria, Ghana, Uganda, Kenya, India and Pakistan. However, migrants from the Caribbean outnumbered all other migrants.

Over time, many Caribbean migrants began to settle down and start families. Their children (who had been born in Britain) regarded themselves not as migrants (because they weren't) but as 'Black British'. By the 1970s a whole generation of young Black Britons – with Caribbean heritage – had emerged. While it is difficult to pin down exactly how many people in Britain have Caribbean ancestry, it is thought to be over a million people. Caribbean migrants and their descendants have had a huge impact on British culture in a number of areas including politics, the arts, music, literature and sport.

▶ **SOURCE D** Viv Anderson, who was the son of African-Caribbean migrants, became the first Black player to represent England at football in a full international match in 1978. In a professional career that lasted over 20 years, he played for clubs such as Nottingham Forest, Arsenal and Manchester United.

▶ **SOURCE E** Michael Fuller was the first Black Chief Constable in the UK. His parents came to the UK from Jamaica in the late 1950s.

▶ **SOURCE F** Johnson Beharry, born in Grenada in the Caribbean, became the first man to win the Victoria Cross (Britain's top bravery medal) since 1982. He received the medal for services to his country in Iraq in 2004. When Queen Elizabeth presented him with the medal she said, 'It's been rather a long time since I awarded one of these'.

▶ **SOURCE G** Diane Abbott became Britain's first Black female MP in 1987. She was born in London to Jamaican parents.

▶ **SOURCE H** Sir Lewis Hamilton, a British world champion racing driver. He is the first Black driver to race in Formula 1. His father is of Grenadian descent.

▶ **SOURCE I** Malorie Blackman is a British writer who held the position of Children's Laureate from 2013 to 2015. The Children's Laureate is a title awarded in the UK once every two years to a writer of children's books to celebrate outstanding achievement. Blackman's parents were both from Barbados and came to Britain as part of the Windrush generation. Her father was a bus driver and her mother worked in a factory.

Over to You

1. Write down three short facts about Claudia Jones.

2. Why did Claudia Jones organise the Caribbean Carnival following the riots in Notting Hill and Nottingham?

3. Look at **Source C**.
   a. Summarise what Corinne Skinner-Carter is talking about.
   b. What impact do you think the contest had on the way some young Caribbean people viewed themselves?

4. You have been asked to nominate a British person of Caribbean heritage for inclusion in a TV programme about 'Great Black Britons'. Produce a short report on the person you have chosen. You should include:
   - who they are
   - a bit of information about their background
   - what they have achieved
   - why you think they should be included.

   You can choose someone mentioned in this chapter, or someone of your own choice.

Migration Nation

3 Have you been learning?

🔄 Quick Knowledge Quiz

Choose the correct answer from the three options:

1. When did the *Empire Windrush* arrive in the UK?
    a June 1945
    b June 1948
    c June 1957

2. In 1948, the UK government passed the British Nationality Act. What were the main changes?
    a all people in the British Empire could have British citizenship and migrate to Britain
    b only people in the Caribbean could have British citizenship and migrate to Britain
    c people living in the British Empire could no longer migrate to Britain

3. By the early 1960s, how many Caribbean-born people were living in England and Wales?
    a 61,000
    b 161,000
    c 1.6 million

4. In which UK city did the 1963 bus boycott take place?
    a Bristol   b Birmingham   c Leeds

5. The government passed the Commonwealth Immigrants Act in 1968. What was the main change in the law?
    a all Commonwealth citizens could live and work in Britain for up to a year
    b Commonwealth citizens could only live and work in Britain if they had a parent or grandparent who was born in Britain, or was a British citizen
    c Commonwealth citizens could not live and work in Britain

6. In 1968, the government passed the Race Relations Act. What was the main change in the law?
    a it was illegal to refuse housing or employment to someone on the basis of their race, colour or national origins
    b it was illegal to discriminate against people on the basis or their race, colour or national origins in shops, restaurants and other public places
    c it was legal to discriminate against people on the basis of their race, colour or national origins

7. In 2012, many Caribbean-born people were faced with deportation to the country of their birth because they did not have certain documents (which they did not know they needed). This became known as what?
    a the Caribbean Scandal
    b the Windrush Problem
    c the Windrush Scandal

8. What was the name of the report that came out of the inquiry into the police's handling of Stephen Lawrence's murder?
    a the Lawrence Report
    b the Macpherson Report
    c the Straw Report

9. In what year was the first Caribbean Carnival held?
    a 1959   b 1969   c 1979

10. Diane Abbott, the UK's first Black female MP, was elected in which year?
    a 1977   b 1987   c 1997

58 Chapter 3: Caribbean migration

Have you been learning?

Analysing a source

Below is a reproduction of one of the pages from the passenger list of the *Empire Windrush*, 1948. Spend some time reading through it, looking at the names, ages, occupations and so on. Then answer the questions that follow.

▼ **SOURCE A** A page from the *Empire Windrush* passenger list, 1948.

NAMES AND DESCRIPTIONS OF BRITISH PASSENGERS

(1) Port of Embarkation	(2) NAMES OF PASSENGERS	(3) AGES OF PASSENGERS								(4) Proposed Address in the United Kingdom	(5) Profession, Occupation or Calling of Passengers	(6) Country of last Permanent Residence
		Accompanied by husband or wife		Not Accompanied by husband or wife		Children between 1 and 12		Infants				
		Males	Females	Males	Females	Males	Females	Males	Females			
505. Kingston	AMOS Kenneth			21						No address.	Welder	Jamaica
506. "	ADOLPHUS Robert			24						"	Carpenter	"
507. "	AUXILLY Allan			25						5 Milton St, Haywood, Lancs.	Mechanic	"
508. "	AQUART Walter			32						22 Hampstead Rd, London	Clerk	"
509. "	ARMSTRONG Joseph			24						No address.	Artist	"
510. "	ANGUS Alva			32						Colonial Welfare Dept., 6 St Martins Place, London	Fitter	"
511. "	ARCHER Gladstone			27						157 Grove St, Liverpool	Hatter	"
512. "	ALLEN Rupert			21						National Service Hostel, 16 Score Street, West Bromwich	Cabinet maker	"
513. "	ANDERSON Ebank			34						16 Sapling Road, Bolton	Engineer	"
514. "	BAUGH Cecil			39						25 Collingham Place, London	Potter	"
515. "	BLAIR Wentworth			26						204 Bute Street	Mechanic	"
516. "	STRANGE Beryl				29					52 Cadogan Square, London	Cook	"
517. "	STEVENS John	58								c/o Lloyds Bank Ltd., Pall Mall, London	Army Officer	England
518. "	" Hamil		57							"	HD	"
520. "	STEWART Vincent	34								Grindlay's Bank Ltd., 54 Parliament Street, London	Engineer	Burma
521. "	" Elizabeth		40							"	HD	"
522. "	" Massey					3				"	–	"
523. "	" Dorinda						1			"	–	"
524. "	" Vreni						11			"	–	"

Immigration Office stamp: 22 JUN 1948 LONDON

1 Background
  a Why did people from the Caribbean choose to come to Britain after the Second World War?
  b What was the *Empire Windrush*?

2 The source
  a Write down some of the job occupations of people on the ship. Note: HD stands for 'Household Domestic' and could mean being a cleaner, servant or a nanny. What sort of industries might they have tried to find work in when they arrived?
  b What does the document reveal about the age range/sex/occupation of the passengers?
  c What can you infer from the source about reasons for coming to Britain?

3 How useful is **Source A** for a historian studying the Windrush generation? What can you learn from it?

4 Imagine you could interview one of the migrants from the Caribbean on the passenger list. Pick one person and write a list of at least five questions you would like to ask them.

Migration Nation

Big Question 6: How has migration changed Britain?

The impact of migration on Britain has been dramatic, influencing everything from the food we eat to the books we read and the freedoms we enjoy. Many, many aspects of life in Britain have been affected by the variety of cultural influences of migrants and the descendants of migrants living in Britain today, and people who have migrated to Britain in the past. The story of migration to Britain is so long, and has had such an impact, that it is hard to imagine what life in Britain would be like without the influence of migration.

Objectives
- Describe ways in which individual migrants, and migrant communities, have changed Britain.
- Analyse the long-term impact of migration on Britain.

A In 1957, there were only 50 Chinese restaurants in the whole country. By 1970, there were 4,000. Chinese food is the most popular takeaway food in Britain. Curry was brought to Britain by migrants from India, Pakistan and Bangladesh and is now Britain's bestselling ready meal.

B We have migrants to thank for some of the most typically British dishes.
- Some parts of the 'full English' breakfast have overseas origins, such as the sausages (Germany), baked beans (America) and black pudding (brought to Britain by European monks).
- Fish and chips: chips came from Belgian or French migrants in the seventeenth century, and fried fish came from Jewish refugees from Spain and Portugal.

C Migration has made its mark on the English language. Everyday words from other places include pal (Romani), shampoo (Hindi) and glitch (Yiddish). Over 200 languages are spoken in Britain today.

D Over the years, many migrants and their descendants have contributed to the cultural life of Britain as musicians, artists and writers. For example:
- Irish-born Oscar Wilde was an author, poet and playwright who lived in Britain. He spent time in prison as he was gay; homosexuality was a crime at that time. *The Picture of Dorian Gray*, published in 1890, had a big impact on literature.
- Samuel Coleridge-Taylor was a well-known composer. He was born in London in 1875, to a white English mother and a Black father from Sierra Leone. His work *Hiawatha's Wedding Feast* was so popular that he went on three tours of the USA.
- Prize-winning authors Andrea Levy and Zadie Smith are of British-Caribbean heritage.
- Sathnam Sanghera is a prize-winning British author and journalist. His parents migrated from India to England in 1968. In 2021, he published a book called *Empireland: How Imperialism Has Shaped Modern Britain*, which aims to educate people about Britain's relationship with the British Empire.
- Michael Omari, better known as Stormzy, is a British rapper. His mother is from Ghana. In 2019 he became the first Black British solo artist to headline Glastonbury Festival. Since 2018, he has provided financial support for two Black students a year to attend Cambridge University.

E Mosques, temples and synagogues are now a common sight in British towns and cities. Bevis Marks Synagogue, built in London in 1701, was Britain's first purpose-built synagogue and the oldest synagogue still in use in the country today. The Shah Jahan Mosque in Woking in Surrey was the first purpose-built mosque in Britain. It opened in 1889 and still welcomes Muslims for worship. The Guru Nanak Gurdwara Sikh Temple in Smethwick, Birmingham (opened in 1961) is the largest gurdwara in Europe.

F Migrants have had a positive impact on the economy. Some are entrepreneurs, establishing new businesses, creating jobs and expanding the British economy. For example, Tesco (Britain's largest supermarket chain) was founded in 1919 by the son of Jewish migrants from Poland.

G Migrants helped to build the canals, railways and roads that were essential to the success of the industrial revolution. This transport network played a large part in Britain's economic success during the period.

H Some say the NHS could not have developed – or survive today – without the contribution of migration. Around 30 per cent of doctors and pharmacists, for example, are of South Asian descent. Many of the first South Asian doctors and nurses who arrived in Britain in the 1950s and 1960s (around 18,000 in total) took jobs in poorer areas of large cities and towns where there was a shortage of doctors.

I Migrants played an important role in campaigns to improve the lives of people in Britain. For example, in the 1800s, Feargus O'Connor (an Irish migrant) and William Cuffay (the son of a formerly enslaved man from St Kitts) campaigned for the right to vote for working people. More recently, Jayaben Desai (born in India in 1933) worked to improve poor working conditions, and Doreen Lawrence (born in Jamaica in 1952) campaigned for important changes in the police force.

Over to You

1. Today, Britain is often described as a 'multicultural' society. Write a sentence or two to explain what you think is meant by the term 'multicultural Britain'.

2. Look at the picture and labels on this page. Make a list of all the ways in which the different influences shown in the diagram relate to your life today.

3. Can you think of other examples of how your life – or life in Britain in general – reflects our multicultural society?

Big Question 7: How has migration been portrayed in the media?

When people talk about 'the media', they are generally referring to the main ways that people receive news, information and entertainment. Interestingly, this has changed over the years. In the 1800s, for example, the main channels of communication were newspapers, books and magazines, while in the modern world it also includes radio, television and the internet. So, over the years, how has migration been portrayed in the media?

Objectives

- Identify how the portrayal of migration has changed over time.
- Examine how the media tries to influence public opinion on migration.

Migration in the media in the 1700s

Throughout history, migrants have been vulnerable to attacks in the media. In the mid-1700s, Jewish migrants found themselves on the receiving end of racist pamphlets (which were like newspapers). The government had proposed a law to allow foreign-born Jewish people who owned property to become full British citizens. Opposition parties were opposed to this and distributed pamphlets which spread lies about Jewish people, accusing them of sacrificing Christian children for their blood. These **antisemitic** lies had been spread in medieval times and were obviously false. However, politicians used them to stir up hatred against Jewish migrants. In the end they were successful and the new law did not pass.

Migration and the media in the 1800s

An early example of the way the media has portrayed migration relates to Jewish migrants who arrived from Eastern Europe and Russia in the late nineteenth century. These migrants were noticeably different to the existing Jewish population in Britain in their culture and language. Most of the new migrants spoke Yiddish and were unable to speak English. Many were already poor when they fled their homes and they had to leave most of their possessions behind, so they had very little when they arrived. They also wore traditional clothes and settled in tight-knit communities.

In general, people in Britain reacted with **prejudice**. Many took against the Jewish migrants, believing in antisemitic stereotypes of Jews. Because Jewish migrants were poor and lived in overcrowded conditions, they were blamed for disease, just as Irish migrants were. Negative views of Jewish people were promoted by the media. For example, Charles Dickens' famous story, *Oliver Twist* (which was published in parts, much like a magazine story today), contains a character based on antisemitic Jewish stereotypes: Fagin is a criminal who profits from sending children out to steal. Many people were persuaded that most Jews were like Fagin.

▼ **SOURCE A** An extract from *Oliver Twist*, which was written between 1837 and 1839. It shows the antisemitic way Dickens presented his Jewish character, Fagin.

'In a frying-pan [...] some sausages were cooking [...] and standing over them was a very old shrivelled Jew, whose villainous-looking and repulsive face was obscured by a quantity of matted red hair.'

Migrants were blamed for social problems

Most migrants settled in poor areas when they first arrived in Britain, living alongside other migrants, often in great hardship and poor conditions. Migrant communities often got the blame for social problems:

- Irish people were blamed for the high crime rates in many towns and cities. Irish navvies (workers who helped build railways and canals) were often seen as drunk and disruptive.

- Jews and Italians were blamed for the spread of cholera, with Italians accused of spreading it in their glass ice cream cones.
- Irish people were blamed for outbreaks of typhus; people called it 'Irish Fever'.

Migrants were also accused of taking jobs from British workers, disrupting strikes and undercutting wages.

▼ **SOURCE B** This cartoon was published in *Punch* magazine in 1852. It shows the overcrowded and unsanitary living conditions in Britain's industrial towns and cities, where many migrant communities found themselves living. Cartoons like this helped to spread negative ideas about people who lived in slums.

Positive stories about migrants

Not all stories in the media about migrants were negative. Mary Seacole, for example, was celebrated for her self-sacrifice as a nurse who served in the Crimean War (1853–1856). Seacole was born in Jamaica in 1805 and moved to Britain in 1821. When war broke out, she travelled to the Crimea (an area in Eastern Europe) where she set up the British Hotel, providing food and clean beds for sick soldiers. After the war she returned to Britain with very little money and a fundraising gala was held for her in 1857; over 80,000 people attended. Her autobiography, *The Wonderful Adventures of Mrs Seacole in Many Lands*, became a bestseller.

Big Question

Key Words

antisemitic   prejudice

▼ **SOURCE C** Mary Seacole (1805–1881) was a nurse and later a bestselling author.

Over to You

1. Define what is meant by the term 'the media'.

2. Read **Source A**.
   a. Who was Fagin?
   b. What can we learn from **Source A** about attitudes towards Jews in the nineteenth century?

3. a. Study **Source B**. What social problems does it show existed in industrial towns and cities in the nineteenth century?
   b. Why do you think people found it easy to make a link between social problems and migrants during this period?

Migration Nation

How has migration been portrayed in the media?

The era of television

Television first became popular in British homes in the 1950s. At the same time, many migrants from former British colonies were arriving in Britain to find work. As you might expect, storylines involving migrants soon began to appear on TV.

TV shows featuring migrants (or their descendants) included comedy shows such as *Till Death Us Do Part* and *Love Thy Neighbour*. These were mainly about racial tension between white British people and their minority ethnic neighbours – and when viewed today seem very outdated and racist (see **Source D**).

Increased visibility

In 1978, *Empire Road* became the first British TV series to be written, acted and directed mainly by Black people. At the time it was seen as an 'ethnic minority' version of *Coronation Street*, with its portrayal of the everyday lives of African-Caribbean and South Asian residents in an ordinary street. However, it only lasted for 15 shows. At the same time, a number of migrants or descendants of migrants began making names for themselves in British TV. Lenny Henry (the son of Jamaican migrants) found fame as a comedian, while Moira Stuart (of African-Caribbean descent) became a well-known newsreader. Another comedy show called *Desmond's* (written by Trix Worrell, who was born in St Lucia, and starring a mainly Black cast) became one of Channel Four's most popular British sitcoms from 1989 to 1994.

In the 1980s and 1990s, more shows began to reflect multicultural Britain to an extent, and actors of different ethnic backgrounds were seen in key roles on TV. However, one criticism was that these characters were often stereotyped. For example, many South Asian characters ran curry houses or were taxi drivers. Also the cast of *EastEnders* is still largely white British, despite East London being one of the most ethnically and culturally diverse parts of the country.

TV and film today

In recent years, TV shows written and performed by British Asians, such as *Goodness Gracious Me* (1998–2001), *Citizen Khan* (2012–present) and *Man Like Mobeen* (2017–present) have been major successes. *The Real McCoy* (1991–1996) and *Famalam* (2017–2020) were both hugely successful sketch shows written by Black Britons. In addition, people of recent migrant heritage have taken lead roles in other major TV shows and films, both in the UK and abroad. Idris Elba (whose parents migrated from Sierra Leone and Ghana) has starred in films such as *Thor* and the TV series *Luther*.

▼ **SOURCE D** *Love Thy Neighbour* ran from 1972 to 1976 and featured two sets of neighbours, one white and one Black. It mirrored to a degree what was happening at the time as recent migrants moved into British cities. The programme showed both the male neighbours using racially offensive language to one another. The show's writer argued it was meant to show humour in racial tension. However, it received negative reviews at the time, even though it was very popular with the public. Today it is rarely repeated, and if it is the show begins with a warning about the racist content.

▶ **SOURCE E** John Boyega (whose parents migrated from Nigeria) starred as Finn in the Star Wars sequel trilogy films (2015-2019).

However, many actors of colour have spoken about the difficulty of landing interesting roles in the UK TV industry. David Harewood (born in

Birmingham to Caribbean migrant parents) is one of the UK's most successful Black actors. However, he has mainly acted in US film and television. In an interview with *The Guardian* in 2021 he said, 'I've never played a leading character on British television […] I had to come to terms with the fact that I was not going to play strong, authoritative characters. […] [In the UK] we're still dealing with people's perceptions of what Black can be.'

Recent migrant portrayals

In recent years, large numbers of migrants have arrived in Britain from many parts of the world: Albanian Kosovans in 1998 and 1999; Somalians from 1991; and Iraqis from 2003, for example. In Syria in 2011, peaceful pro-democracy demonstrations were violently stopped by the government and a civil war began. Hundreds of thousands of people have died, and more than a quarter of the country's population has fled the fighting. Some of the people who escaped Syria have come (or have tried to come) to Britain. The media has played an important role in how the existing population has viewed migrants. The media can encourage people to be fearful, using language designed to shock, for example talking about 'vast numbers' of migrants who will 'flood' Britain and 'sponge' off the state by claiming money from the government as benefits. Some newspapers, for example, have a reputation for promoting anti-immigration messages. However, some sections of the media can also encourage people to have sympathy for those who have lost everything in war or famine and are seeking a safe place to raise their children. At times, the same newspaper can have a particular view about migrants from one part of the world, and an opposite view about migrants from somewhere else.

Significance

Why was Empire Road a significant TV programme in the portrayal of migration in the media?

Big Question

▼ **SOURCE F** Front pages from the *Daily Express* and its Sunday edition, the *Sunday Express*. Both front pages relate to migration to Britain, but they are presented in very different ways.

▼ **SOURCE G** From a 2016 report by the University of Oxford's Migration Observatory on migration in the media.

'Where do the public get their ideas about immigration? One frequently cited source – besides day-to-day contact with immigrants themselves, or what friends and work colleagues might say – is the media. […] The role of media in shaping public opinion is not clear-cut. It has often been observed that the press is good at setting the agenda – telling readers what to think about – although there is an ongoing debate about the extent to which media coverage either causes or simply reflects the views of its audiences on the topics it discusses.'

Over to You

1 Suggest reasons why some TV programmes began to feature stories about migration from the 1950s.

2 Look at **Source D**.
   a *Love Thy Neighbour* was very popular at the time of its release. What might that show about attitudes towards migration and race at this time?
   b Today, this show is very rarely repeated on TV. Suggest reasons why.

3 Describe how the media can play an important role in how people view migrants or the descendents of migrants. Use the information on these pages, and **Sources F** and **G** to help you.

4.1 Britain and South Asia

South Asia is part of the continent of Asia. It includes countries such as Bangladesh, India, Pakistan and Sri Lanka. It is sometimes known as the 'Indian subcontinent' and for many years this vast area was under British control as part of the British Empire. As a consequence, the links between Britain and South Asia go back hundreds of years. This chapter explores the link between people from this region and Britain. It will examine the reasons why people from South Asia came to Britain, how people reacted to their arrival, and the impact they made – both at the time and continuing to this day.

Objectives

- Define 'lascars' and 'ayahs'.
- Examine how lascars and ayahs relate to the reasons why many South Asians first came to Britain in the 1700s and 1800s.
- Explore the experience and contribution of a number of South Asian migrants in Britain up until the early twentieth century.

Lascars

During the 1700s and 1800s, more and more of South Asia came under the control of Britain. Large parts of this area were known as 'British India' and it remained part of the British Empire until 1947. From the earliest days of British rule, South Asians began to migrate to Britain. Many worked as cooks, deckhands and sailors on board ships bringing goods to Britain. These South Asian sailors (called **lascars**) were paid less than British sailors and were often treated badly. Between voyages many lascars settled near British ports (such as London, Liverpool, Cardiff and Glasgow) and took on other jobs. Some settled in Britain permanently because they didn't want to return to work on a ship with low pay and poor treatment. Many ran lodging houses for other sailors, set up cafes or tea shops in the places they settled, or became market traders.

▶ **SOURCE A** Three lascars on board a ship, pictured in the early 1900s.

Ayahs

Sailors weren't the only South Asian immigrants to settle in Britain during the time of empire. There were also **ayahs** (nannies and nursemaids) and servants of wealthy British families who had lived in South Asia but decided to return home to Britain. In fact, by the 1800s, it was estimated that there were around 40,000 South Asians in Britain – mainly lascars, but also ayahs, servants, students, officials, doctors, tourists and businesspeople. After working for families in Britain, some ayahs lost their jobs. This happened so often that, in 1891, the Ayahs' Home was set up in East London to support them.

▼ **SOURCE B** Two ayahs from Madras (now Chennai), India, photographed in Glasgow, 1925.

Chapter 4: South Asian migration

Studying in Britain

Some Indians migrated to Britain temporarily, to study at British universities. Having a degree from a British university made it easier to get a job with the Indian government when they returned home. Cornelia Sorabji (see **Source C**) travelled to Britain to attend Oxford University in 1889. She was the first woman to study law there. While in Britain, she fought for the right to sit exams with male students at the end of her course, and for equal rights for women at the university.

▶ **SOURCE C**
Cornelia Sorabji (1866–1954). Sorabji returned to India in 1893 and became the first woman to practise law in India.

▼ **SOURCE D** Mohandas Gandhi, who went on to be a leading figure in the Indian independence movement, was a law student in London in the late 1800s. He is pictured here (bottom right) with members of the Vegetarian Society in 1890.

▶ **SOURCE E** Sake Dean Mahomed (1759–1851), a Bengali traveller and entrepreneur, migrated to Britain in the early 1800s. In 1810, Mahomed opened a restaurant in London called the Hindoostane Coffee House, serving traditional Indian food. Some historians suggest that this was Britain's first Indian restaurant. Then, in 1814, Mahomed moved to Brighton and opened an indoor bathhouse. The baths became very popular; even royalty visited. Some people credit Mahomed with introducing shampooing to Britain!

Key Words   lascar   ayah

Fact

In 1794, Mahomed published a book called *The Travels of Dean Mahomet*. It was the first book written in English by an Indian author.

▶ **SOURCE F** Kumar Shri Ranjitsinhji ('Ranji') was born in India in 1872 and migrated to Britain in 1888. He captained Sussex County Cricket Team for nearly 20 years and in 1896 became the first Indian to represent England at cricket – and scored a century in his first Test! He scored another century in his first 'away' Test in another country too, a feat not repeated for over 100 years.

▶ **SOURCE G** Sophia Duleep Singh, the daughter of an Indian Sikh prince and his African-German wife, was born in Suffolk in 1876. She is pictured here selling the *Suffragette* newspaper outside Hampton Court Palace. Singh was prominent in the fight for women's rights – in particular the right to vote – in the early 1900s.

Over to You

1. a What is meant by the term 'South Asia'?
   b In what way is Britain linked to South Asia?

2. a Define:
      i lascar   ii ayah
   b Explain why lascars and ayahs settled in Britain.

3. a Authors have difficult decisions to make when selecting people to appear in textbooks. Explain why you think Sake Dean Mahomed, Kumar Shri Ranjitsinhji and Cornelia Sorabji have been chosen to appear on these pages.
   b Can you suggest reasons why this textbook doesn't include lots of details about individual ayahs and lascars?

Migration Nation

4.2A The South Asian experience

People from South Asia have been migrating to Britain for hundreds of years. They came as students, doctors, servants, businesspeople and nannies (ayahs) too. But it was in the 1950s and 1960s that very large numbers of South Asian migrants began coming to Britain. In 1951, for example, there were around 40,000 people of South Asian descent in Britain, and by 1961 there were over 110,000. So why did so many South Asians migrate to Britain? What did they do when they got here? What were attitudes to this migration like at the time?

Objectives

- Outline why many South Asians chose to move to Britain in the 1950s and 1960s.
- Explore the experiences of the groups that came.

Fact ✓

By 1971, the number of migrants from South Asia had reached around 400,000 people. This is a significant number of people – however, it equates to only about one per cent of the total population of Britain at that time. Today around five and a half million people of South Asian descent live in Britain.

Fact ✓

In Britain, the term 'Asian' usually refers to people who trace their ancestry to the Indian subcontinent (South Asia). However, in other places, such as Australia and the USA, the term 'Asian' usually refers to people who trace their ancestry to East Asia or Southeast Asia.

Why migrate?

There were many reasons why thousands of South Asians came to settle in Britain after the Second World War:

- When India gained independence from Britain in 1947, it was divided into different countries by the British: India and Pakistan. This partition led to violence, as whole populations moved across the dividing lines. Some people came to Britain to escape this situation.
- The people of many South Asian countries, including India, Pakistan and Bangladesh, were entitled to a British passport because these places had been part of the British Empire. So they had the right to come and live in Britain.
- Some places in South Asia suffered from cyclones, floods, famines and terrible poverty. Many people living in these areas saw **emigration** as their only hope.

However, the vast majority of South Asians who came to Britain in the 1950s and 1960s came for one reason – jobs! Some of the immigrants had professional qualifications – for example, many were doctors and nurses who came to work in Britain's hospitals. But lots were unskilled workers who came to get a job in one of Britain's key industries, many of which were experiencing a shortage of workers after the war. Soon, thousands of South Asians had taken jobs at Wolf's Rubber Factory in Southall, near London, or at Heathrow Airport. There were also lots of jobs at iron foundries in Birmingham, steelworks in Scunthorpe and Sheffield, and textile mills in northern towns such as Bolton and Bradford.

▼ **SOURCE A** A worker of South Asian Sikh origin on the assembly line at the Ford Factory, Dagenham, 1978.

Connections

The Second World War connects the growth in many migrant communities in Britain. One of the key reasons why people from South Asia, the Caribbean and Eastern Europe migrated to Britain after the war was because there was a chronic shortage of workers. Britain was trying to rebuild and it needed people to fill jobs in farming, transport, engineering, mining, textile work, brick making, steel manufacturing and the new National Health Service.

▶ **SOURCE B** Young Indian women, who had recently arrived in London from Calcutta (Kolkata), India in September 1957.

▼ **INTERPRETATION C** Gilli Salvat talks about travelling from India to England in 1948. Her family was one of the first of many migrant families from India and Pakistan who were encouraged to come to Britain with promises of work. Note that 'coloured' was a word used to describe Asian and Black people. It is considered offensive today.

'I remember standing on the rail of the boat as it pulled away from India and my parents were both crying and crying, and India was getting smaller and smaller [...] I didn't really understand why they were crying [...] We docked in Tilbury [about 20 miles from central London], and it was a really grey day [...] and then we stayed in an immigrant camp, which was in the basement of this church, near Selfridges [in London]. They had all the men and boys in one part and all the women and girls, all on these iron cots [...] Nobody wanted children, nobody wanted coloureds [...] My dad just walked all over London. The only shop that we knew about was Harrods [an expensive shop in central London], because that's what had been in all the magazines [...] They took us to Harrods and bought me and my sister coats, because we didn't have any warm clothing. People were so unused to seeing black people in the street, we used to be walking along Oxford Street and people used to stop and just stare at us [...] I went to school [...] and in about three weeks I changed my accent, and I started learning to survive.'

Key Word   emigration

▼ **INTERPRETATION D** Mohamed Zaman Khan talking about his experiences upon arrival in Britain. He refers to his contribution fighting for Britain in the Second World War.

'When I first arrived the local people generally didn't like us. Once I remember being confronted by a white man telling me, "you lot are good for nothing. You come over here, take our jobs and we don't like you". I told him that it was my country too, I had fought for it and if we had been late getting to the battlefront this country would have been in the hands of the Germans.'

Over to You

1. Make a list of reasons why many South Asians came to settle in Britain after the Second World War.

2. Complete the following sentences with an accurate term:
   a. India gained independence from Britain in…
   b. By 1971, the number of people of South Asian descent living in Britain was around…
   c. Many South Asians had jobs in steelworks in…
   d. In Bolton, Bradford and Manchester, many South Asians worked in…

3. Describe the problems facing South Asians who migrated to Britain after the Second World War. Use the information in the main text and **Interpretations C** and **D**.

Interpretation Analysis

How useful are **Interpretations C** and **D** to a historian studying the problems facing South Asian migrants to Britain?

Migration Nation

4.2B The South Asian experience

Life in Britain

The experience of starting a new life in Britain varied enormously. Some migrants were treated with kindness by the existing population and adapted to life in a new country quickly. They found jobs, worked hard, started families, and achieved a great deal. Others found life extremely tough. They struggled to be accepted and found it hard to adapt to the new way of life. Many missed home, suffered racist abuse, and experienced unequal opportunities in housing and jobs.

Sometimes, the qualifications gained by migrants in South Asia were not recognised in Britain. As a result, well-qualified professionals such as teachers, medics and engineers sometimes had to work in lower-skilled jobs in factories and foundries when they arrived. Look at **Interpretations E, F** and **G**. They illustrate some of the varied experiences of South Asian immigrants in Britain.

▼ **INTERPRETATION E** Abdul Aslam, born in Kashmir, remembers his early schooldays in Bradford, England.

'I came to England in 1966, I was 14 years old and I started school. We were used to living in bright sunlight and there was no sunlight. I came in July and even in July you hardly see any sun. [...] My English was not too bad at that time and so I went to a mixed school, Belle Vue Boys High School in Bradford. There were about 12 to 14 in the whole class, we were all foreigners. It was a bit difficult because the teachers didn't call us by names they used to call us, "you brown one".'

▼ **INTERPRETATION F** Mr Laxman, who migrated from India in 1957, remembers the first few years after his arrival in Leicester, England.

'The weather was unacceptable at first. Slowly ... slowly got used to it. [...] We were happy we got a job. Living nice and comfortable. We got together on special days like Diwali and Independence Day. [...] When I came at first we got our spices from India. It took about 2 or 3 months by ship. A cargo ship to Tilbury Docks. We wrote to our parents to send for us. Sometimes we received it a bit late. A parcel was sent to us and a letter received from the shipping company to say it had arrived. There was only one shop in Leicester that carried a few Indian spices. Very expensive. It was easier and better quality coming from India. People were very nice. We spoke very little English. Very friendly. People all mixed together. Never any trouble in fifty years.'

▼ **INTERPRETATION G** Sonali Bhattacharyya recalls her parents' experiences. They moved to Britain from India in the late 1960s.

'My mother was highly educated, having completed her MA in Bengali literature at Kolkata University. She had worked as a deputy headmistress before moving to Britain. Despite her experience and qualifications, Manju had great difficulty finding employment. [...] This was a common experience of many immigrants, no matter how qualified; they were often forced to take the most menial [basic], low-paid jobs on offer. For example in West Yorkshire, 50–80% of mill workers were South Asian. My mother was no different.'

Changing opportunities

In the 1970s and 1980s many of Britain's factories, mills and steelworks closed down. As a result, thousands of people in Britain lost their jobs – including a lot of South Asian migrants and their descendants. However, many South Asians were determined to keep working hard, and a lot of them decided to set up their own small businesses. In 1974, only eight per cent of South Asians were self-employed, but by 1991 that figure had risen to 26 per cent. For example, by the early 1990s, it was estimated that around 70 per cent of sweet shops, grocers and newsagents in Britain were owned by South Asians.

Discrimination and racism

South Asians in Britain have faced discrimination and racism for many years, right up to the present day. In the 1970s and 1980s, for example, an openly racist political group called the National Front violently targeted British Asian and other

Meanwhile... 1974

Jayaben Desai was born in India in 1933 and then lived in Tanzania. When South Asians were made unwelcome in newly independent Tanzania, she moved to London and went to work at the Grunwick Film Processing Laboratories in 1974. Desai resigned after being forced to work overtime, and in protest at the way her fellow female workers (most of them migrants) were made to work long hours for low wages, and could not go to the toilet without asking permission. Desai organised a strike to protest against the poor working conditions. The Grunwick Dispute, which was widely supported, went on for two years and included a hunger strike. Although the factory owners ignored the findings of an enquiry to reinstate the sacked workers and improve conditions, the strike is seen as a model for industrial action.

minority and migrant groups. Sometimes the attacks led to murder. In 1978, a young Bangladeshi man named Altab Ali was stabbed to death in a racially motivated killing in London. Ten days after his death, 7,000 people marched behind his coffin through central London, calling on the government to address racism. They took Ali's coffin to 10 Downing Street, the home of the Prime Minister. Soon, anti-racist groups began to develop (known as Asian Youth Movements) to fight discrimination within their communities. Well-known anti-racist groups such as the Anti-Nazi League and the Newham Youth Movement were formed at this time.

The next generation

Many South Asian migrants came to Britain alone at first. Most were male, and many left their wives and families behind. Most of these men hoped to return to South Asia after a few years. However, in the early 1960s, a new law meant that it would be more difficult for them to return to Britain at a later date if they wanted to. As a result, many men decided to stay and asked their families to come to Britain to join them. Some of the men married local British women. In time, as their children were born in Britain, a 'second generation' of South Asians emerged. A government report of 1960 recorded a total of 34,000 Indian children and 5,000 Pakistani children in Britain – and around 64 per cent of them had been born in Britain. This next generation often regard themselves as British Asians (see **Source H**).

▼ **SOURCE H** Sukhjinder Singh, a British Asian student from the West Midlands, speaking in 2010. His mother was born in Britain and his father was born in India. All his grandparents were Indian migrants in the 1960s.

> 'I'm British – end of story. I was born in Britain and I've lived all my life here. I dress like I'm British, sound like I'm British, have a mix of mates from all cultures – but I certainly see myself as a Brit first, a British Asian yes, but I'm British first and foremost.'

Over to You

1. What is meant by the term 'second generation'?

2. a Describe how the experiences of South Asian migrants varied.
   b Suggest reasons why the experiences varied.

3. Read **Interpretations E, F** and **G**.
   a Briefly summarise what has been said in each interpretation.
   b How useful is each interpretation for a historian studying the experiences of South Asian migrants in Britain?
   c If you could speak to each of the people writing these interpretations, what would you ask them and why?

Knowledge and Understanding

Describe the impact of the murder of Altab Ali in 1978.

4.3 South Asian people in East Africa

South Asians did not just migrate to Britain from South Asia. It might surprise you to know that, in the 1960s and 1970s, thousands of people of South Asian descent migrated to Britain from East Africa – in particular, from Kenya and Uganda. Why did they come? What were they doing in East Africa in the first place? What were the reactions to their arrival?

Objectives

- Explore why East African Asians came to Britain in the 1960s and 1970s.
- Examine some of the experiences of East African Asians.

East African Asians

In the late 1800s, thousands of South Asians moved from British India to Uganda and Kenya in East Africa. At the time, these countries were under British control as part of the British Empire. Many migrants moved there as part of the indenture system. This meant that migrants would agree to work for a period of five years in another country in return for a basic wage and transport to their new workplace. The worker was to be returned at the end of the period of service to their country of origin. Over 30,000 South Asians moved to Kenya and Uganda under the indenture system to help build railways, bridges and roads. Some went home when the work was finished, but thousands stayed and their descendants went on to play a vital part in the East African economy as traders, business owners, medical professionals and shopkeepers. They became known as 'Kenyan Asians' and 'Ugandan Asians'.

▼ **SOURCE A** The 1,000-kilometre-long Uganda Railway in British East Africa was built mainly by indentured workers from India, like the ones pictured here.

Leaving Africa

When Uganda and Kenya gained independence from Britain in the 1960s, their new governments wanted to create a strong sense of national identity for Africans. So, both Kenya and Uganda began a programme of 'Africanisation'. This meant that the countries' new African leaders tried to ensure that key government, business and medical positions were taken by Africans. As a result, the lives of South Asians who had settled in Kenya and Uganda because of the British Empire were made very difficult, and many left.

A new life in Britain

Between 1965 and 1967, around 23,000 South Asians left Kenya. Then, in 1972, the Ugandan government gave the country's South Asian population 90 days to leave the country. As a result, around 50,000 South Asians were forced to leave Uganda. Some went to Canada, Malaysia and the USA, but the vast majority (about 30,000) came to Britain. The Prime Minister at the time, Edward Heath, said that Britain had a moral responsibility to help people who had British passports. The government created the Uganda Resettlement Board to help local councils find buildings and homes into which refugee families could move.

Initially, there was some concern about the arrival of a large number of migrants. Leicester City Council, for example, was worried that it would not be able to cope with so many migrants and placed adverts in Ugandan newspapers urging them to stay away from Leicester. The advert warned that there were no houses and no jobs, and that the schools were full. It read, 'In your own interests and those of your family you should … not come to Leicester.' However, the advert had the opposite effect. Many Ugandan Asians who read the advert thought they were being told not to come to Leicester because it was a wealthy city, so they decided it was the perfect place to settle! Eventually, Leicester City Council made efforts to help the new arrivals settle in. For example, they brought forward the opening date of a new school – now called Judgemeadow Community College – so that children from Uganda could continue with their education.

Eventually public sympathy towards the migrants grew in Britain as stories of the way they were treated in their former homes were published in British newspapers. Many church groups, charities and individuals helped them by providing food and shelter.

> **Later on... 2012**
>
> In 2012, Leicester City Council officially apologised for the 1972 advert.

▼ **SOURCE B** Some of the first Ugandan Asians arriving at Stansted Airport, September 1972.

▼ **INTERPRETATION C** Tahera Aanchawan came to Britain in 1972. Like other South Asians who fled Uganda, she was allowed to bring just two suitcases and £50 with her.

'My mother took the head of her sewing machine and wrapped it up in a quilt [...] She was a seamstress [someone who sews, makes and mends clothes] and for her that would be a way of earning a living.'

Key Word   'Africanisation'

▼ **INTERPRETATION D** From a BBC online article called *A History of Leicester* by Jeevan Panesar, written in 2005.

'In Leicester you will not escape the culture Asian migrants have brought with them. Melton Road, infamously referred to as the Golden Mile, will spoil you for choice with the countless gold jewellery shops, Indian restaurants and colourful sari shops. In the heart of Evington you will find one of the city's biggest Mosques; merging distinct Eastern architecture to the English buildings that have their own unique history. Asians have brought their passion for sport with them too; the madness when India are playing in a cricket match, the hockey clubs and even kabaddi! This culture is never more present than at the time of the Asian festivals; Diwali, Eid and Vaisakhi. The strength and community in these celebrations shows that no matter where they go, they will take their identity with them.'

▼ **INTERPRETATION E** Adapted from an interview with Nik Kotecha who arrived from Uganda in 1972, aged 16.

'When we came here people weren't amazed to see us because there were quite a few arriving at the same time. There was a refugee centre called "Helping People Out" and we used to queue there for blankets and things like that, and people were alright – probably because we didn't understand them and they didn't understand us. They couldn't understand our English and we couldn't understand them. But I don't think people found it difficult to settle in places where there were already lots of Indian people.'

Over to You

1. What is meant by the term 'indenture system'?
2. Why did East African Asians come to Britain in the 1960s and 1970s?
3. Did the British welcome migrants from East Africa? Explain your answer.
4. Describe the experience of East African Asian migrants in Leicester.

Causation

Explain why so many people from South Asia migrated to Uganda and Kenya in the 1800s.

Migration Nation

4.4 South Asian people in Britain today

Many of the South Asian migrants who arrived in the 1950s, 1960s and 1970s made Britain their home. Their children, grandchildren and great-grandchildren were born in Britain – and are British. They are often referred to as British Asians. Today, around 9.3 per cent of the population identify as Asian/British Asian. Mostly, they are of Indian, Pakistani, Bangladeshi and Sri Lankan descent, but descendants of other South Asian areas (such as Nepal or the Maldives) have settled in Britain too. The main religions of British Asians are Islam, Hinduism and Sikhism, but other faiths represented include Christianity, Buddhism, Jainism and Zoroastrianism. The impact of South Asian migrants, and their children and grandchildren, on life in Britain has been immense, and reaches all sorts of areas – the arts and entertainment, business and industry, science, sport and politics. This chapter looks at just some examples.

Objectives

- Examine the impact of South Asian migrants, and their descendants, on modern Britain.

Healthcare

In healthcare, around 30 per cent of doctors and pharmacists are of South Asian descent. Many of the first South Asian doctors and nurses who arrived in Britain in the 1950s and 1960s (around 18,000 in total) took jobs in poorer areas of large cities and towns where there was a shortage of doctors (see **Source A**).

▼ **SOURCE A** A British nurse of South Asian descent, 1965.

▼ **SOURCE B** Dr Navina Evans, NHS England's chief workforce officer, writing in 2022.

'We are proud of who we are, the NHS has always been built by people of many backgrounds coming together and people of South Asian heritage have played a fundamental role in our nation's history and development. Our contribution is immense, and it will continue to be so. We serve this nation with respect and dignity and ask to be treated with such in return.'

Politics and activism

There is a long history of British South Asian involvement in politics, with three MPs of South Asian origin being elected in the nineteenth century. However, until the late twentieth century, British Asian MPs were very rare. Since then, there have been more MPs of South Asian heritage. Most notably, Sadiq Khan (of Pakistani descent) became Mayor of London in 2016, Rishi Sunak (of East African Asian descent) became the first British Asian Prime Minister of the United Kingdom in October 2022, and Humza Yousaf (of Pakistani and East African Asian descent) became First Minister of Scotland in 2023. British South Asians have also been hugely effective campaigners for social justice. For example, Jayaben Desai led the influential Grunwick Dispute calling for better workers' rights in 1976 (see page 71).

▶ **SOURCE C** Rishi Sunak became the first British Asian Prime Minister of the UK in 2022.

Chapter 4: South Asian migration

Food

The influence of South Asian migration is hugely evident in what people in Britain eat – and the way they eat. Although the first Indian restaurant was opened in 1810, it wasn't until after the Second World War that South Asian restaurants really took off. To start with, 'Indian' restaurants catered to homesick migrants, but soon they became popular with people of all backgrounds. In 1950, there were six 'Indian' restaurants in the UK. By 1970 that number was 2,000, and today it is over 12,000.

Arts and the media

In arts and the media, many British Asians have made their mark. Writers such as Salman Rushdie, Monica Ali, Meera Syal and Sathnam Sanghera have topped the best seller lists and won literary awards. British Asian comedy shows and dramas have won prime time TV slots and numerous TV awards. In recent years, films such as *Bend it Like Beckham* and Oscar-winning *Slumdog Millionaire* have enjoyed huge success. In 2013, Amol Rajan became the editor of the *Independent*, making him the first person of South Asian heritage to edit a British national newspaper in over a century.

Meanwhile... 2020

Today, despite strict laws controlling racist behaviour and discrimination, race-hate crimes still occur. In recent years, hate crimes directed at both South and East Asian communities have increased, and a 2020 survey found that around 30 per cent of South Asians had experienced racist language directed at them on multiple occasions.

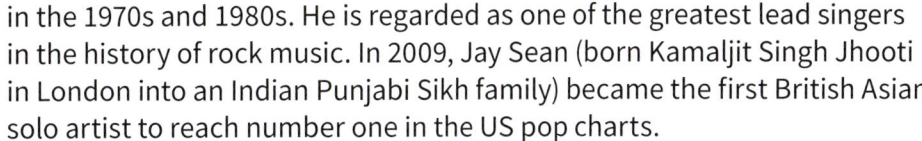

▶ **SOURCE D** Freddie Mercury performing in 1985.

Music

One of the first British Asian musicians to gain worldwide fame was Freddie Mercury (born Farrokh Bulsara in East Africa to Indian parents). He was the lead singer of rock band Queen who had massive hits in the 1970s and 1980s. He is regarded as one of the greatest lead singers in the history of rock music. In 2009, Jay Sean (born Kamaljit Singh Jhooti in London into an Indian Punjabi Sikh family) became the first British Asian solo artist to reach number one in the US pop charts.

Sport

Descendants of South Asian migrants have played a key role in British sport for many years. For example, Nasser Hussain (born in India to an Indian father and an English mother), Monty Panesar (of Indian descent), Moeen Ali and Adil Rashid (both of Pakistani descent) have each represented England's cricket team. In the 1930s, Mohammed Salim (from Bengal) became the first South Asian to play for a European football club when he played for Celtic F.C.

Business

Some South Asian migrants and British Asians are entrepreneurs, establishing new businesses, creating jobs, and expanding the British economy in industries such as steel manufacturing, clothing and fashion, food, property and IT. For example, Tilda Rice is an example of a successful business established in Britain by Ugandan Asian migrants. The Thakrar family came to Britain in the 1970s. They realised that migrants were looking for a high-quality aromatic basmati rice, just like the rice they were used to eating before they moved to Britain. Today, Tilda Rice sells in more than 50 countries worldwide.

Over to You

You have been asked to nominate a British person of South Asian heritage for inclusion in a TV programme about South Asian people in Britain. Produce a short report on the person you have chosen. You should include:
- who they are
- a bit of information about their background
- what they have achieved
- why you think they should be included.

You can choose someone mentioned in this chapter, or someone of your own choice.

Significance

How significant was South Asian migration for British society after the Second World War?

4 Have you been learning?

Quick Knowledge Quiz

Choose the correct answer from the three options:

1. Which countries are part of South Asia?
   a. India, Pakistan, Bangladesh and Sri Lanka
   b. Pakistan, China and Malaysia
   c. India, Pakistan, Bangladesh and Thailand

2. What was an ayah?
   a. a British nanny working in India
   b. a nanny or nursemaid from Asia working for Europeans
   c. any servant of South Asian origin working for Europeans

3. What is Sophia Duleep Singh known for?
   a. she was the first Indian female MP
   b. she was a campaigner for Indian independence
   c. she was a suffragette, campaigning for womens' right to vote

4. By the early 1970s, how many people of South Asian descent lived in Britain?
   a. 40,000
   b. 400,000
   c. 4 million

5. How many people of South Asian descent live in Britain today?
   a. 500,000
   b. 5.5 million
   c. 10 million

6. In 1972, people of South Asian origin were forced to flee which African country?
   a. Uganda
   b. Ghana
   c. Nigeria

7. South Asian migrants from Africa settled in many places in Britain. Which of the following cities tried to put them off by advertising in newspapers?
   a. Leeds
   b. Liverpool
   c. Leicester

8. In which year was Altab Ali murdered in a racist attack?
   a. 1968
   b. 1978
   c. 1988

9. What percentage of NHS doctors and pharmacists are of South Asian descent?
   a. 10 per cent
   b. 30 per cent
   c. 50 per cent

10. Rishi Sunak, the first UK Prime minister of South Asian descent became Prime Minister in which year?
    a. 2018
    b. 2020
    c. 2022

Have you been learning?

Understanding academic texts

Academic text is a type of text or writing that is written by experts and professionals in a particular area or on a specific topic. It is written in a formal way, and isn't usually aimed at students who might be reading it in school. However, this doesn't mean students can't have a go at understanding it.

The following article was written in 2011 by Professor Susheila Nasta (an author and Professor at the University of London), Dr Florian Stadtler (a writer and Senior Lecturer at the University of Exeter) and Rozina Visram (an author of several books on the history of India and Pakistan). Read the article carefully and use the labels to help you answer the questions.

1. Describe the work of a pedlar.
2. How did pedlars, such as Buttha Mahomed, provide an important service to their customers?
3. What do you think the authors mean when they write that the Asian settlers 'became integrated within their local geographical communities'?
4. What do you think the authors mean when they say 'equality proved illusory' for the settlers?
5. Based on your knowledge of other settlers, what problems might they have faced?

---

run-down: A word used to describe something that is in poor condition and is falling apart.

pedlars: People who go from place to place selling small items along the street or from door to door.

working-class: The social group made up of people who do manual, physical work. Often working-class people don't own much property.

clientele: A group of customers who use your services or buy goods from you regularly.

consumer goods: Everyday items sold to consumers for their use or enjoyment.

on credit: A method of paying for goods or services at a later time, usually paying interest as well as the original money.

domestic households: The homes of ordinary people.

descendants: People who are related to you and who live after you, such as a grandchild.

integrated: When something is 'integrated', it means it has become part of it.

Read about Sake Dean Mahomed on page 67.

Born in India, Shapurji Saklatvala was the first person of Indian heritage to become a British Member of Parliament (MP).

inter-racial marriages: Marriages that take place between people of different ethnic and/or cultural backgrounds.

equality proved illusory: Equality means when all the members of a society or group have the same status, rights, and opportunities. Illusory means when something isn't real. Here the authors are saying that the South Asian settlers weren't really treated equally.

After World War One, a new group of working-class Asians arrived who often worked as pedlars. Many lived in poor areas with run-down housing. With a suitcase full of items of light clothing – shirts, scarves, ties and aprons – they travelled miles in all-weather to build up a clientele. Asian pedlars were a familiar sight in many parts of Britain. They bought and sold consumer goods – often on credit – to areas where shops were few, providing a service on the doorstep. Buttha Mahomed, for example, came to Britain in 1931 and began work peddling goods to domestic households. From Glasgow he travelled all along the west coast of Scotland, arriving in Stornoway, Isle of Lewis, where he settled and continued to work as a pedlar. His descendants still live on the island.

These early Asian settlers set up clubs and societies, and established places of worship – gurdwaras, mosques and temples. As they became integrated within their local geographical communities, Asians from working-class and middle-class backgrounds, like Sake Dean Mahomed and Shapurji Saklatvala, entered inter-racial marriages [...] Although they were officially British citizens, equality proved illusory.

Migration Nation

Big Question 8: Which migrant groups have arrived in Britain in recent years?

A migrant is a person who moves from one place to another. Some migrants leave their country because they choose to ('voluntary migration'), while others leave because of war or persecution, for example ('forced migration'). Sometimes people who have been forced to leave a place are called 'refugees'. However, another group of people sometimes move from one place to another, but are called 'asylum seekers'. So, what is the key difference between a refugee and an asylum seeker? Why did refugees and asylum seekers come to Britain in the modern period? What was life like for them when they arrived?

Objectives

- Outline why some of the migrants arriving in Britain in the modern period have fled their homes.
- Describe the experiences of refugees and asylum seekers in Britain in the modern period.

A history of moving to Britain

Britain welcomed Protestant migrants during the 1500s, 1600s and 1700s, and became home to greater numbers of Jewish and Irish migrants in the eighteenth, nineteenth and twentieth centuries. After the Second World War, many

▶ **MAP A** A map showing where some of the people who arrived in Britain from the 1970s onwards came from.

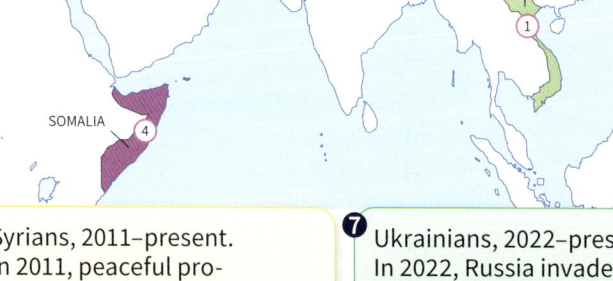

❶ Vietnamese, 1975–1992. People fled South Vietnam because of political unrest after the Vietnam War. Most Vietnamese 'boat people', as they came to be known, left in 1978 and 1979, but refugees continued to leave Vietnam until the early 1990s.

❷ Bosniaks, 1992–1995. The Bosnian War took place in Bosnia and Herzegovina from 1992 to 1995, between the three ethnic groups living in the country: Serbians, Croats and Bosniaks (Bosnian Muslims). During the conflict, the Serbians committed **genocide** and many Bosnians, most of whom were Bosniaks, fled the country.

❸ Albanian Kosovans, 1998–1999. The Kosovo War took place in Kosovo between 1998 and 1999, between two ethnic groups living in the country: Serbians and Albanians. During the conflict, the Serbians committed **atrocities** against the Albanians, many of whom fled the country.

❹ Somalians, 1991–present. There has been a civil war between different groups in Somalia since 1991. There have also been severe droughts in the country throughout the last 30 years. War and starvation have forced many to leave Somalia to seek safety elsewhere in the world.

❺ Iraqis, 2003–present. In 2003, the USA and its allies (including Britain) invaded Iraq; the Iraq War lasted until 2011. The war devastated the country and terrorism flourished in the region. Many people have fled to escape the problems in Iraq.

❻ Syrians, 2011–present. In 2011, peaceful pro-democracy demonstrations were violently put down by the Syrian government and a civil war began. Hundreds of thousands of people have died, and more than a quarter of the country's population has fled the fighting.

❼ Ukrainians, 2022–present. In 2022, Russia invaded Ukraine. Millions of Ukrainians left their homes to escape the fighting. Most tried to find safety in neighbouring countries such as Poland, as well as travelling further to countries such as Germany and Britain.

people came to Britain from the countries of the British Empire and the Commonwealth. Most of these people came to find work. However, from the 1970s, large numbers of people have arrived as a result of conflict and political unrest. These people are migrating (because they are moving from one place to another), but they are usually referred to as refugees and asylum seekers.

- Refugees are people who have been forced to leave their homes to escape war, persecution or a natural disaster. Refugees have similar rights to British citizens and, after five years, can apply to live permanently in Britain.
- Asylum seekers are people who have asked a government to recognise their status as refugees and are waiting to hear the outcome of their application. They have limited rights – for example, they are not allowed to work.

Both refugees and asylum seekers are in Britain legally. Many refugees and asylum seekers choose to come to Britain because they already have relatives or friends in the country. Also, the English language is more widely spoken by migrants than any other European language, and they feel this may help them settle in Britain. Furthermore, there is a belief among some that the living conditions in Britain will be better than in some other European countries.

How has the British government responded?

Over the years, the British government has tended to focus on restricting the number of migrants settling in Britain, including the number of refugees. For example:

- In the 1990s, a series of Acts of Parliament reduced the support available to people seeking asylum in Britain.
- In 2005, the government introduced a citizenship test, the 'Life in the UK' test. People must score at least 75 per cent to be able to apply for citizenship. The test has been widely criticised because it contains questions that many people who were born and live in Britain struggle to answer.
- In recent years, some people seeking asylum in Britain are held in detention centres while they wait for the government to decide if they can stay in the country as refugees. Asylum claims are meant to be decided within six months but can take much longer.

Big Question

Key Words   genocide   atrocity

The British government has been both criticised and praised for its response to different refugee crises. Some feel the government does not do enough, while others believe the government gets too involved. For example, 2,500 Bosnians escaping the Bosnian War, 4,000 Kosovans escaping the Kosovan War, and 20,000 Syrians escaping the civil war in Syria have come to Britain under government resettlement schemes. Also, after the Russian invasion of Ukraine, the government promised to give thousands of people shelter and support, and offered money to people in Britain to host Ukrainian refugees in their homes. However, the British government has been criticised for hosting too few refugees; by way of comparison, Germany is home to 560,000 Syrian refugees. Also, from 2022 to 2023, around 160,000 Ukrainian refugees settled in Britain, while over a million went to Germany.

▼ **INTERPRETATION B** A Sudanese woman talking in *The Heritage and Contributions of Refugees to the UK – a Credit to the Nation*, published by Refugee Week in 2015.

'The word refugee is a label. As soon as you say the word, you put a bad picture in someone's mind. There is confusion about who is genuine and who isn't. People think you come here just to claim benefits but they don't see we had better lives at home. We had jobs, status, qualifications which aren't recognised here.'

Over to You

1. Explain the difference between a refugee and an asylum seeker.
2. Why have refugees and asylum seekers come to Britain in the late twentieth and early twenty-first centuries? Give a variety of reasons.
3. List countries that refugees and asylum seekers have come from. Do you know of any more?

Knowledge and Understanding

Describe two ways the British government responded to refugees and asylum seekers in the late twentieth and early twenty-first centuries.

5.1A Eastern European migration to Britain before and after the Second World War

As the name suggests, Eastern Europe is the eastern part of the continent of Europe. Any definition of Eastern Europe usually includes European countries to the east of Germany, Austria and Italy. Eastern Europe traditionally includes countries such as Poland, Bulgaria, Czech Republic (also known as Czechia), Hungary, Romania, Russia, and Croatia, for example. Migrants from Eastern Europe (and their descendants) have been present in Britain for hundreds of years, but usually only in small numbers. However, in the late twentieth and early twenty-first centuries, there was a large increase in migration to Britain from Eastern Europe. This chapter explores why this happened, what the experience was like for Eastern Europeans, and why this large-scale migration went into decline after 2016.

> **Objectives**
> - Define Eastern Europe.
> - Examine reasons why Eastern European migrants came to Britain up to, during, and after the Second World War.

Early migration from Eastern Europe

There is a long history of migration from Eastern Europe to Britain. For example, in the late 1500s, Polish grain merchants began settling in England (mainly in London), and lots of Hungarian students came to study at English and Scottish universities in the 1600s. In the 1700s, Polish Protestants fled religious persecution in their homeland and settled in the Soho district of London – around 'Poland Street'. In the late 1800s, large numbers of Jewish migrants arrived from Eastern Europe, mainly Russia. They were escaping poverty and pogroms – the organised and deliberate killing of a particular ethnic group. Perhaps the best-known migrant to arrive from Eastern Europe at this time was Michael Marks. He arrived in Britain in 1882, after escaping anti-Jewish persecution in modern-day Belarus. In 1894, he teamed up with Englishman Tom Spencer and founded one of the best-known high street stores in the world. By 1901, it was recorded that there were just over 86,000 Eastern Europeans in England and Wales, and a further 10,000 in Scotland.

Eastern Europe and the Second World War

In the years before the Second World War, many people from Eastern Europe (particularly Jews) fled from places under Nazi control. The Kindertransport (see pages 24–25), for example, was the organised rescue of around 10,000 children from Nazi-controlled territory that took place between November 1938 and September 1939. Many of the children arrived from Germany and Austria, but thousands were also rescued from Czechoslovakia (modern day Czech Republic and Slovakia) and Poland. The children were allowed to enter Britain without visas or passports, and were placed in foster homes, schools, and on farms. Many parents of the children who had been rescued were killed during the war, so lots of them chose to stay in Britain and build new lives because they had no family to go home to.

Many adults also fled Nazi-occupied territory to help Britain in the war against Germany's forces. For example, when Czechoslovakia was occupied by the Nazis, many Czechs and Slovaks left their homeland to fight abroad. About 6,500 men moved to Britain to serve as airmen, as parachutists or in the army. Hundreds of Czech and Slovak women served in the women's version of the British Royal Air Force (known as the WAAF) and the British Army Auxiliary Corps, which was the women's version of the British Army. They worked in offices, workshops and hospitals, as well as in departments for mapping, weather analysis and code-breaking.

SOURCE A Czech women serving in the British Army Auxiliary Corps during the Second World War.

SOURCE B A British poster issued by the Royal Air Force in 1941. It shows allied airforce emblems and portraits of fighter pilots from abroad who had fled to Britain to help fight Germany. Note the pilots from Eastern Europe.

In recognition of this contribution, the government passed the Polish Resettlement Act in 1947. It stated that Poles who had served under British command during the war, and their dependents who had come to Britain since September 1939, would be supported in Britain. Over 100,000 Poles settled in Britain after the act was passed. This was the first time the government had passed a law that allowed such a large number of migrants to settle. The 1951 census recorded just over 162,000 Poles living in Britain.

SOURCE C Members of 303 Squadron, a predominantly Polish squadron that played an important role in the Battle of Britain.

SOURCE D The Polish War Memorial near RAF Northolt, London (where seven Polish fighter squadrons were based in the war). Over 18,000 men and women served in the Polish squadrons of the RAF during the war, and over 2,000 died.

The Polish Resettlement Act

Many Polish pilots were also welcomed into the Royal Air Force and played an important role in the Battle of Britain in 1940. Also, Polish battleships joined Britain's Royal Navy, and Polish soldiers served in the army and were part of the ground force that defeated the Germans.

Over to You

1. Define 'Eastern Europe'.
2. List reasons why many Eastern Europeans migrated from their homelands in the years up to and including the Second World War.
3. In what ways did Eastern European migrants contribute to the war effort?

Migration Nation 81

5.1B Eastern European migration to Britain before and after the Second World War

European Voluntary Workers scheme

Polish people were allowed to stay in Britain after the war – but the country was still very short of workers. Large areas of many cities had been destroyed by enemy bombing and the programme of rebuilding needed workers. There were also jobs available in factories, mines, hospitals and transport networks, for example. People from both the Caribbean (see pages 46–49) and Eastern Europe were invited to Britain to take up these jobs.

The workers from Eastern Europe were invited as part of the European Voluntary Workers (EVW) scheme. In total around 90,000 Eastern Europeans arrived in the first few years after the war, mainly from Ukraine, Poland and Latvia.

In general, the migrants had similar pay and rights to British workers, but could not change jobs without permission from the government. Many also experienced discrimination – for example, they were often refused promotion and were the first to be fired if there were any job cuts.

When the migrants arrived, they were housed in one of around resettlement 200 camps located all over Britain. Polish migrants under the Polish resettlement scheme also lived in these camps. The camps were often on army bases and the 'homes' given to people were simple, basic, poorly heated huts. Inspectors at the camps also criticised the schooling the children received. However, the migrants made the best of their situation and built churches, schools and leisure facilities. They formed choirs, bands and sports teams and kept their own culture and heritage alive with traditional processions, dances and festivals. At one camp, in Melton Mowbray, Leicestershire, there were 420 adults and nearly 150 children and babies. Nearly all the adults worked locally at either the ironworks or steelworks, or the clothing, shoe or boot factories.

Over time, the migrants moved out of the EVW camps and began to live in the local towns and cities. By the mid-1960s there were only around 50 camps left, and the last few closed in the early 1970s. Large Eastern European communities built up around Britain, including in London, and other places such as Wiltshire, Leicestershire and Shropshire. Some Eastern European migrants married British people and adopted the culture and traditions of British society. Others were determined to keep their Eastern European identities and culture alive and established clubs, societies, churches and parades that reflected their original homeland.

▶ **SOURCE E** Polish women hanging out laundry at a resettlement camp in the 1940s.

▼ **SOURCE F** A young Polish couple on their wedding day at Melton Mowbray resettlement camp in the early 1950s.

▼ **SOURCE H** A Yugoslavian family outside their home at a resettlement camp, 1968. Notice how the residents of the camp had made improvements to their homes and gardens since the early days of the camps after the war.

▼ **INTERPRETATION G** Historian Agata Blaszczyk on conditions in Polish resettlement camps. A Nissen hut is an arched-style steel building. You can see examples in **Sources E**, **F** and **H**.

'The camps were generally in remote locations with Nissen huts or poor-quality dwellings, each occupied by more than one family. The huts were equipped with electric lights and heated by slow combustion stoves but had poor natural ventilation and light. However, for the first generation of Poles they became a symbol of stability, and for the second generation the camps would remain in their memory as happy places, full of freedom.'

Fact

When Germany invaded Poland in 1939, many Polish universities closed. Some students, university lecturers and researchers came to Britain and were hosted by British universities. This allowed the students to carry on with their studies. In total, four Polish departments were set up at British universities: medicine at Edinburgh (1941), architecture at Liverpool (1942), veterinary studies at Edinburgh (1943) and law at Oxford (1944).

Over to You

1. What was the European Voluntary Workers scheme?
2. What can you learn from **Source E** and **Interpretation G** about conditions in resettlement camps?
3. How useful is **Source H** to a historian studying the European Voluntary Workers scheme?

Causation

Outline two reasons why the number of people of Eastern European origin living in Britain rose during and after the Second World War.

5.2 The EU and Eastern European migration

After the horrors of the Second World War, when European neighbours had been enemies, European leaders saw that things had to change. They were determined to avoid another large-scale war, and felt that future peace was far more likely if differences in language, culture and history were put aside, and countries worked together. Rather than compete as rivals, they would join forces where possible to develop Europe peacefully. This led to the formation of the European Economic Community (EEC) in 1957. This was later renamed the European Union (EU). What did membership of the EEC and EU mean for Eastern European migration to Britain?

Objectives

- Describe why and how the EU was formed.
- Assess how membership of the EU made an impact on Eastern European migration to Britain.

The early years

In the 1950s, Britain had strong ties with the many countries that were still part of the British Empire, so it did not join the European Economic Community (EEC) when it was established. However, as more and more countries gained independence from Britain and it became clear that the EEC was an economic success, Britain changed its mind, joining in 1973.

By the late 1980s, there were 12 countries in the EEC. In 1992, the member states signed the Maastricht Treaty and the EEC became the European Union (EU). The treaty established the idea of 'European citizenship' and it meant that, for the first time, citizens of one member state had the right to work and settle in another member state. During the 1990s and 2000s, membership of the EU grew rapidly.

Meanwhile... 1950

By 1950, around 100,000 Hungarians, Ukrainians, Yugoslavs, Estonians, Latvians and Lithuanians, who had fled from Russian communist rule, had also settled in Britain.

Expansion and migration

Over the years, migration to Britain from EU countries steadily increased. In the 1970s, for example, around 20,000 EU citizens per year entered Britain, rising to about 60,000 per year in the late 1990s. However, the greatest increase in EU migration to Britain took place soon after the EU expanded, allowing many more countries to join.

In 2004, ten countries joined the EU on the same day. Eight of these were in Eastern Europe: the Czech Republic, Estonia, Hungary, Latvia, Lithuania, Poland, Slovakia and Slovenia. Three years later, two more Eastern European countries joined – Romania and Bulgaria. Generally speaking, these countries were poorer than many of the existing EU countries, so the wealthier countries such as Britain, Germany,

▼ **MAP A** The evolution of the European Union, showing when member states joined by decade.

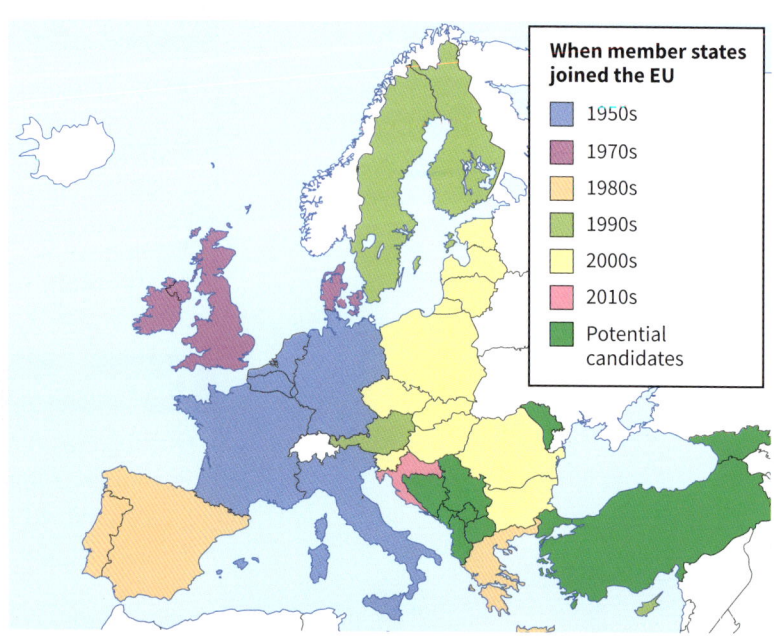

France and Ireland attracted people from these new EU member states as there were more job opportunities. Also, there had been a tradition of European migration to Britain going back many years, particularly around the time of the Second World War, so many migrants were drawn to Britain as a result. Between 2004 and 2008, around 750,000 Eastern European migrants came to Britain.

The experience of Eastern European migrants in Britain

Many Eastern European EU migrants found jobs on farms, on building sites, in shops and in hotels. They also took up highly skilled positions as vets and dentists, for example. They often earned far more than they did in their home countries. The economy also benefited because they spent some of their wages in shops in Britain and bought goods such as clothing, food, electrical items and so on. Many started new businesses and opened shops, and also paid taxes, which went to the British government.

Migration from EU countries has caused debate at local and national levels. Many believe it was good for Britain, and that it enriched the country and individual communities. There is also evidence to suggest that there is no link between immigration and unemployment. However, in some places, some people felt that the number of people arriving put local services, such as schools and housing, under pressure. In some cases, this was because the government used out-of-date population data to plan key services and underestimated the number of migrants who would come. Some sections of the media also promoted anti-immigration messages.

▼ **SOURCE C** From an article in the *Daily Telegraph*, 2013.

'Eastern European immigrants add far more to the UK economy than they take out and should not face restrictions on their movements, foreign ministers from EU accession countries have said.

Migrants from central and eastern parts of Europe are younger and "economically more active" than the average British worker, the politicians said in a joint statement.

They boost the UK economy by contributing more in taxes and spending than is claimed back in social benefits, it was claimed.'

▼ **TABLE B** The largest group of new EU migrants into Britain at this time were from Poland. Using Poland as an example, this table outlines the impacts of this migration on both Britain and Poland.

Impacts on Britain (the host country)	Impacts on Poland (the source country)
• Many immigrants are young, hard-working, well-educated and motivated. • Many fill job shortages in farm work, building and healthcare, as well as highly skilled professional jobs. • Some towns and villages experienced higher numbers of migrants than others, leading to some concerns about the impact on local services, such as schools. • Local and national economy benefits because of the immigrants renting houses, buying goods and services, and paying taxes.	• Money sent back to Poland helps the Polish economy. • There are fewer unemployed people in Poland. • There are fewer skilled workers in Poland (such as dentists and plumbers). • Poland's population is ageing because so many younger workers are leaving. This also means the Polish government does not receive tax from these people.

Over to You

1 Explain why many Europeans wanted to increase cooperation between countries in the 1950s.

2 a Write the following dates out in the correct chronological order: 1992, 2004, 1957, 1973.

b Next to each date, write out an important fact in the history of the EU.

3 Write two short paragraphs of no more than 75 words each. In the first, explain some of the impacts of European migration on the UK. In the other, explain some of the impacts on the countries the migrants are leaving.

5.3 Eastern Europeans in Britain today

Between 2004 and 2008, around 750,000 Eastern European migrants came to Britain. This period saw the most rapid increase in Eastern European migration. For the next few years after 2008, the number of migrants from Eastern Europe coming to settle in Britain was varied. In some years, tens of thousands of people would migrate to Britain, while at other times, the numbers would be relatively low. So, what causes these fluctuations? Why do some European migrants choose to stay, while others leave? And why, after 2016, did more Eastern European migrants leave Britain than arrive?

Objectives

- Examine why fluctuations in migration from Eastern Europe have taken place.
- Assess the impact of Brexit on Eastern European migration.

Ups and downs

The majority of people who have come to Britain from Eastern Europe in the last few decades have been economic migrants – migrants who have moved to find better jobs or better living conditions. Economic migrants are voluntary migrants. However, sometimes things change in the country the migrants have left, which causes them to return. For example, in the late 2000s, the economies of some Eastern European countries improved. In Poland there were plenty of jobs in construction, technology and financial services. Also, the economy in Britain wasn't doing so well and there were fewer jobs available. As a result, many Polish migrants decided to head back to Poland. In fact, in 2009, for the first time since 2004, more Eastern European migrants left Britain than arrived. However, over the next few years, the economy in Britain improved and Eastern European migration increased again. It is important to note that during this time, many of those who stayed in the UK built up their lives here, progressing at work and buying homes.

Meanwhile... 2007

Some Eastern European countries encourage the migrants that have left to return home. In 2007 there was a '*Wracaj do Polski*' ('Come Back to Poland') campaign, and in 2015 the Polish government again began a campaign to persuade Poles in Britain to go back and benefit Poland instead.

Brexit

In recent years, the event that has had a major impact on Eastern European migration is Brexit. In June 2016, a national vote, known as a referendum, was held in the UK to decide whether Britain should remain part of the EU. Fifty-two per cent voted to leave the EU (in a process that became known as 'Brexit', meaning 'British Exit') while 48 per cent voted to remain. Migration from the EU has been given as one of the main reasons why many voters opted to leave. In one survey, a third of 'leave voters' said their main reason for voting for Brexit was to control migration. Eventually, after nearly four years of debate, the UK finally left the EU on 31 January 2020.

Since this date, people from the EU can no longer move freely to Britain. EU citizens who want to settle in Britain are now subject to a points-based immigration system that citizens of other countries are subject to. EU citizens who had already lived in Britain for five years had to apply for 'settled status', and EU citizens who had lived in Britain for fewer than five years had to apply for 'pre-settled status'. Many felt that the process was unnecessarily complicated, with some elderly people finding it particularly difficult to understand.

The long-term impacts of Brexit are unclear. However, since the Brexit vote in 2016 there has been a steep decline in Eastern European migration to Britain. Many reasons have been suggested to explain the decline; for example:

- There are fewer jobs as the British economy struggles after Brexit and the Covid-19 pandemic.
- There is a feeling among some migrants that they are not as welcome in Britain as they once were.

One estimate suggests that between 100,000 and 300,000 Eastern Europeans left Britain in 2020. Another suggests that Eastern European migration is now a *negative* figure. In other words, more Eastern Europeans are leaving Britain than arriving. Indeed, many businesses are reporting that fewer EU citizens coming to Britain is making it hard for them to find enough workers. For example, before 2016, almost all of the 75,000 seasonal workers who gather the fruit and vegetable harvest in the UK were from Eastern Europe. There are also shortages of workers in hotels, cafes, restaurants and the transport industry.

▼ **SOURCE A** Migrant workers from Eastern Europe planting lettuces in Suffolk.

Meanwhile... 2022

In 2022, Russia invaded Ukraine. Millions of Ukrainians left their homes to escape the fighting. Most tried to find safety in neighbouring countries such as Poland. Others travelled further to countries such as Germany and the UK. In the first year of the conflict, around 150,000 Ukrainian refugees arrived in the UK.

▼ **SOURCE B** Katrin Muirhead is an Estonian who works in a hotel in the Scottish Highlands. She moved to Britain in 2006 and married a Scottish man in 2010. She has had to apply to stay in Britain since Brexit.

'I came to Britain to work and live when Britain was part of the EU. I created a life and home. Since Brexit I have had to apply for settled status to stay in Britain. It would be very difficult, almost impossible, for me to move to Britain now if I wanted as there are too many restrictions. When Britain was part of the EU it felt like we were all part of a big family, but since Brexit it feels like we are isolated and alone.'

▼ **SOURCE C** From a 2021 article in the *Financial Times* about the impact of Eastern European migration on the UK.

'Marcin Poltorak's story is typical of the experiences of many who arrived in Britain after 2004. He joined friends at the Clitheroe slaughterhouse, sleeping on a mattress on the floor of a shared house and sending most of his earnings back home. "It was the hardest I have ever worked," he recalls.

By 2009, he had bought a house on a former council estate in Preston, a city of about 142,000 in the north of England. It contains touches of his homeland, such as wooden furniture and carvings from the Tatra mountains. His wife Alicja, who spoke no English when she arrived, now works in a sewing factory where almost the entire staff are Polish.

The couple have two children, both born in the UK. "In England you work hard, you get a house, car, a foreign holiday once a year," he says. "It has been so good for me."

But the atmosphere around the Brexit vote soured the mood, admits Poltorak, who has worked as a go-between for the police and Preston's Eastern European migrant community. As well as experiencing abuse in the streets, he recalls youths damaging a car and even setting fire to a hedge. "Brexit was a sad moment," he says.'

Over to You

1. Why, in 2009, did more Eastern European migrants leave Britain than arrive?
2. a. Define 'Brexit'.
   b. Describe a short-term impact that Brexit has had on Eastern European migration.
3. Study **Sources B** and **C**. How far do the sources agree with each other?

Source Analysis

What can be learned from **Sources B** and **C** about the impact of Brexit on Eastern European migrants?

Migration Nation 87

5 Have you been learning?

Quick Knowledge Quiz

Choose the correct answer from the three options:

1. During the Second World War, 18,000 Polish men and women contributed to the British war effort in what way?
   a by serving in the British Army
   b by serving in the Royal Navy
   c by serving in the Royal Air Force

2. After the Second World War, people from Eastern Europe were invited by the UK government to settle in Britain to fill jobs as there was a shortage of workers. What was this government scheme called?
   a the Eastern European Migration Scheme
   b the European Voluntary Workers Scheme
   c the Polish Resettlement Scheme

3. How many people from Eastern Europe settled in the UK under this scheme in the years immediately following the Second World War?
   a 9,000
   b 45,000
   c 90,000

4. In 1992, the European Economic Community became the European Union (EU). What were the new rules on migration?
   a all EU citizens had the right to live and work in other EU countries
   b all EU citizens had the right to live and work in other EU countries for a year
   c EU citizens had the right to move anywhere in the world to work

5. Eight Eastern European countries (the Czech Republic, Estonia, Hungary, Latvia, Lithuania, Poland, Slovakia and Slovenia) joined the EU on the same day in which year?
   a 1980
   b 1992
   c 2004

6. How many Eastern European people migrated to Britain between 2004 and 2008?
   a 75,000
   b 750,0000
   c 2 million

7. In 2007, the Polish Government began a campaign called *Wracaj do Polski*. What was the aim of this campaign?
   a to encourage Polish people to migrate to the UK
   b to encourage Polish people to stay in Poland
   c to encourage Polish people working abroad to return to Poland

8. In 2016, most of the UK's seasonal workers who gathered the fruit and vegetable harvest were from Eastern Europe. How many people did these jobs?
   a 10,000
   b 25,000
   c 75,000

9. In which year did the UK vote to leave the European Union?
   a 2012
   b 2016
   c 2020

10. Which of the following statements is true?
    a Migration to the UK from Eastern Europe rose every year between 2004 and 2020.
    b Migration to the UK from Eastern Europe has fallen every year between 2004 and 2020.
    c Migration to the UK from Eastern Europe has gone up and down between 2004 and 2020.

Chapter 5: Eastern European migration

Have you been learning?

Odd two out

Here are five paragraphs about European migration to the UK. Each paragraph has two errors. One is a spelling mistake, and the other is a factual error. When you have spotted the mistakes, write each paragraph out correctly.

1. In the late-1700s, large numbers of Jewish migrants arrived in Britain from Easten Europe, mainly Russia. They were escaping poverty and pogroms. Pogroms are the organised and deliberate killing of a particular ethnic group.

2. The Kindertransport was the organised rescue of around 10,000 Jewish adults from Nazi-controlled territory that took place between November 1938 and September 1939. Many of the children arrived from Germany and Austria, but thousands were also rescued from Eastern European countries such as Czechoslovakia and Poland.

3. During the First World War, hundreds of Czech and Slovak women served in the women's version of the British Royal Air Force (known as the WAAF). Many Polish pilots were also welcomed into the Royal Air Forse and played an important role in the Battle of Britain in 1940.

4. After the war, workers from Eastern Europe were invited as part of the European Voluntary Workers (EVW) scheme. In total around 90,000 Eastern Europeans arrived in the first few years after the war, mainly from Ukraine, Ireland and Latvia.

5. In 2014, ten countries joined the European Union (EU) on the same day – including several Eastern European nations such as Poland, Hungary, the Czech Republic and Slovakia. Three years later, two more Eastern European countries joined – Romanea and Bulgaria.

Thinking about your learning

This is a quote from a best-selling book by Robert Winder called *Bloody Foreigners: The Story of Immigration to Britain* (2013). Here he tries to sum up the 'immigration story':

> 'Immigration is a story. And, like all the best stories, it has happy moments as well as sad ones, comedies as well as tragedies. The list of shameful episodes is long, and growing longer every day. But there are uplifting tales too – of people remaking their lives. The immigrant experience is not uniform: some people come hurriedly, as refugees; others to seek their fortunes. Many find heartache, but many have prospered. It has been a momentous adventure both for each individual and for the nation they have settled in and reshaped'.

1. From your studies of migration, can you think of any 'shameful episodes'?

2. Can you think of any times when migrants have 'come hurriedly, as refugees'?

3. Can you think of any examples of where people have come to 'seek their fortunes'?

4. In what ways have some migrants found 'heartache' while others 'have prospered'?

5. List ways in which immigration has 'reshaped' Britain.

Big Question 9: Why is migration a controversial topic?

For centuries, people have had very strong opinions about migration. There were debates and arguments in the 1800s, for example, when large groups of Jewish and Irish migrants arrived in Britain. Even earlier, in the seventeenth century, many people objected to the arrival of Huguenot migrants from France, while others saw the value of their skills and contribution to British society. In short, there is nothing new about the 'migration debate'. So why does this topic arouse such strong emotions?

Objectives
- Outline key arguments in the 'migration debate'.
- Examine how data can be used to support different views.

The key issue

Today, in homes, schools and workplaces all over Britain, the migration debate is regularly discussed, argued over and even shouted about. Migration-related stories and reports often appear in newspapers and online, and they feature heavily in TV news programmes and documentaries. For decades, public surveys have often named migration as one of Britain's 'most important issues'.

The reason why migration is such a controversial topic is rather straightforward – it is a very **divisive** issue. In other words, some people believe migration is a problem that needs to be dealt with, while others see migration as positively contributing to society. A 2022 survey by one of the biggest market research firms in the world highlighted this. It showed that 29 per cent of people interviewed felt that migration had a negative impact on Britain, while 46 per cent felt migration had a positive effect. The rest of the people surveyed were unsure.

The key arguments

There are many views on the topic of migration – some are positive, some are negative. Below are some of the views that someone who is against migration (or believes it should be more tightly controlled) might hold:

- New migrants to the country take jobs from British workers – and if they haven't got a job, they claim benefits from the government.
- Britain cannot afford to take in all the migrants from other countries that want to be here. Britain is already crowded – and its housing, education and health services cannot take the strain of even more people.
- Migration is making Britain lose its national identity. Migrants isolate themselves in their own communities and some don't learn English.

However, as in any debate, other people might have views that challenge those who are against migration:

- New migrants do not 'steal jobs' from British workers. They often take the tough, low-paid jobs that most British workers won't do – or they make up shortages in highly skilled professions such as medicine.
- Most migrants are of working age so they pay tax and spend money on goods and services like everyone else. As taxpayers, they're entitled to use Britain's health service and education system, just like the existing population are … and those without jobs should be able to go to a doctor for free on the NHS, just like an unemployed British person can.
- People should be free to move somewhere else for a better life.
- Britain's national identity is always changing. The idea that migrants are 'ruining' it is not true. Britain's identity has been built up over the centuries and lots of cultures have contributed to it. Migrants have added to Britain's culture and made huge contributions to all areas of life.

Big Question

Key Word: divisive

▼ **SOURCE A** David Cameron, the UK's Prime Minister from 2010 to 2016, speaking in 2011.

'It [migration] has placed real pressures on communities up and down the country. Not just pressures on schools, housing and healthcare [...] but social pressures too. Because [...] real communities are bound by common experiences. And these bonds can take time. So real integration takes time.

That's why, when there have been significant numbers of new people arriving in neighbourhoods [...] perhaps not able to speak the same language as those living there [...] on occasions not really wanting or even willing to integrate [...] that has created a kind of discomfort and disjointedness in some neighbourhoods.'

▼ **SOURCE B** From the same speech as **Source A** by Prime Minister David Cameron, 2011.

'Our country has benefitted immeasurably from immigration. Go into any hospital and you'll find people from Uganda, India and Pakistan who are caring for our sick. Go into schools and universities and you'll find teachers from all over the world. Go to almost any high street in the country and you'll find entrepreneurs from overseas who are not just adding to the local economy but playing a part in local life. Charities, financial services, fashion, food, music – all these sectors are what they are because of immigration. So yes, immigrants make a huge contribution to Britain.'

▼ **SOURCE C** Adapted from a BBC article about a report on migration, 2008. Community cohesion refers to how well different groups get on with each other within the community.

'Rapid immigration has damaged community relations in parts of England, a report by a House of Commons committee says.

In three areas with high immigration – Peterborough, Burnley, and Barking and Dagenham – community cohesion is among the lowest in the country, the MPs say.

The report said there was "significant public anxiety" over issues such as pressure on public services.'

▼ **SOURCE D** From a 2013 article on migration by Professor Bart Édes, a specialist in international development.

'They [migrants] clean clothes, homes, offices and streets; construct buildings; staff fishing vessels; tend to the children of white-collar professionals; pick crops; wash dishes; stock shelves; and carry heavy loads. Migrant workers perform dirty, difficult and dangerous jobs that people in their host country don't wish to do.'

▼ **SOURCE E** From a BBC report about a study on immigration carried out by University College London, 2013.

'The study said recent immigrants were less likely to claim benefits and live in social housing than people born in Britain.

The authors said rather than being a "drain", their contribution had been "remarkably strong". [...]

Immigrants who arrived after 1999 were 45 per cent less likely to receive state benefits or tax credits than UK natives in the period 2000–2011.'

Over to You

1. Choose four sources from these pages. For each one say whether the source supports (is in favour of) migration to the UK, or whether it is against (is quite negative about) migration to the UK. For each source, explain in your own words the point that the source is trying to make.

2. a. List three arguments that someone might give if they were against migration to the UK.
   b. Suggest three answers that a person who believes migration is a positive thing might use in response.

3. Why do you think migration is such a controversial topic?

Source Analysis

Look at **Sources A** and **B**. How useful are these sources to a historian studying the migration debate?

Why is migration a controversial topic?

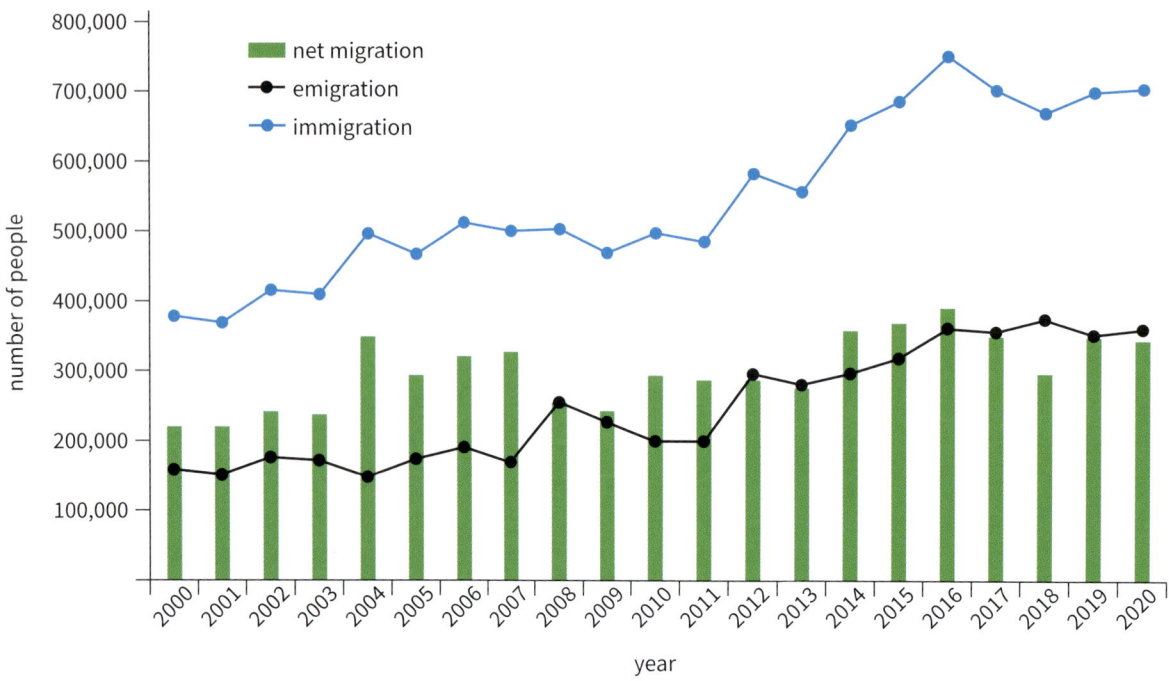

SOURCE F Migration to and from the UK, 2000–2020.

The key facts and figures

Britain has a long history of immigration (people coming into the country) and emigration (people leaving). Up until the 1980s there were more people moving out of Britain (to places like Australia, Canada, Spain and New Zealand) than coming into the country. Since then, things have changed.

As **Source F** shows, since the early 2000s there has been a steady increase in the number of people moving to the UK. In 2010, for example, around 500,000 people settled in the UK (the blue line), and 200,000 left (the black line). This left a net figure of 300,000 people – so Britain's population increased by 300,000 due to migration in 2010.

Fact ✓

Net migration is the difference between the number of immigrants and the number of emigrants. So, if 500,000 people move to a country, and 100,000 leave – the net migration figure is 400,000. However, if 500,000 people emigrate, and 100,000 move to the same country, the net migration figure is *minus* 400,000. In other words, more people are leaving than arriving.

Undocumented migrants

One of the most controversial aspects of the migration debate is the issue of undocumented migrants. Undocumented migrants (sometimes referred to as illegal immigrants) are people who come to Britain by illegal means (smuggled into the country hidden in lorries or small boats, for example). They have no proper documentation and have not applied to be here through official channels. This may be as they have had to leave their homes suddenly without their personal documents such as passports or may have had them taken from them. Most experts agree that it is difficult to estimate how many undocumented migrants there are. In some areas, it is the issue of illegal immigration that sparks the fiercest debate.

SOURCE G In recent years, the UK has started to use high-tech equipment to detect migrants coming to Britain by illegal means. This image was taken by an x-ray scanner at a British port. You can see people hidden in a lorry.

Using statistics

As you might imagine, people (especially journalists and politicians) seize on these yearly immigration figures and can skilfully twist the numbers to back up whatever point they want to make. For example, if a politician wanted to use the figures in **Source F** to argue that migration is 'out of control', they might say that 'the graph shows a rapid rise in immigration over the last 20 years, which is a result of letting more people into Britain'. However, someone wishing to argue that immigration is 'under control' might say that 'since 2016 migration to Britain has dropped. In fact, net migration has dropped from 2016'.

Different interpretations of the same report

Official reports can be interpreted in different ways. For example, read carefully the following report on migration.

> **Migration report**
>
> A new report by an independent organisation that advises the government has revealed some fascinating information on the impact of migration. Figures calculated by the organisation showed that the average adult migrant from an EU country contributes £2,300 more per year in taxes than the average UK resident.
>
> Migrants from some countries contribute more than others – but even the lower-paid EU workers are making a net public contribution. In all, the report states that EU migrants paid £4.7 billion more in taxes than they took out in benefits and public services.
>
> However, the report also points out that, when averaged out, the figures are not particularly large. Averaged out over the whole of the UK-born population, it amounts to an extra £1.70 a week, per person.

It is possible for people (and the media) to interpret this report differently. Some newspaper and media commentators might report this in a positive way. They might write that 'migrants make a huge £4.7 billion contribution to the UK' and emphasise all the financial benefits of migration. However, it would not be difficult to imagine that some newspapers and media commentators might not be so positive about the report. They might write that 'migrants only contribute £1.70 per week' and focus on the fact that the contribution is not particularly large. To some extent, both statements are true – but they are selecting the parts of the report they wish to emphasise and the message they want to give. This might be a result of their personal feelings – and this happens a lot in society today.

Over to You

1. a What is the difference between immigration and emigration?
   b Define 'net migration'. Use an example from **Source F** in your answer.

2. Look at **Source F**. How might this chart be used to show:
   a that immigration to the UK is 'out of control and rising'?
   b that immigration to the UK 'has peaked'?

3. Why do you think migration figures are used by different groups in different ways?

Source Analysis

How useful is **Source F** to a historian studying migration in the UK from 2000 to 2020?

Glossary

'Africanisation' the process of giving control of government and business to Africans after countries in Africa gained their independence from the British Empire

antisemitic hostile to, or prejudiced, against Jewish people or people of Jewish heritage

antisemitism hatred for, and persecution of, Jewish people as an ethnic, religious or racial group

asylum seeker person who has asked a government to recognise their status as a refugee and is waiting to hear the outcome of their application so they can be legally recognised as a refugee

atrocity an extremely wicked or cruel act, often involving violence

ayah a nurse or nanny employed by Europeans in India and other British colonies

boycott refusal to buy goods or services from a person or organisation as a protest

Caribbean a region consisting of the Caribbean Sea, its islands and the surrounding coasts

colony an area or country controlled by another country; for example, Britain controlled a huge number of colonies, which made up its empire

'colour bar' racist system that meant that non-white people were denied the opportunities, particularly the job opportunities, that were available to white people

Commonwealth voluntary organisation of independent countries, most of which were once part of the British Empire; countries in the Commonwealth have close cultural, sporting and trade links to Britain

divisive something that causes disagreements that separate people into opposing groups

emigrant person who moves out of a country to live in another country

emigration the process of leaving a country to settle in another country

empire a collection of areas of land (or whole countries) that are ruled over and controlled by one leading or 'mother' country

exploited when a person is used and treated badly by others who seek to gain something from them

genocide The deliberate killing of a large number of people from a particular nation or ethnic group with the aim of completely destroying that group

Holocaust The systematic, state-sponsored persecution and murder of six million European Jews by the Nazis, their allies and collaborators

hunter-gatherer A person who lived mainly by hunting animals, fishing, and harvesting wild plants

immigrant person who moves into a country from another country

institutional racism policies, rules, and practices that are part of the way an organisation works that result in (and support) continued unfair advantage to some people and unfair or harmful treatment of others based on race

interned when a person is put in prison for political or military reasons

lascar a sailor or army servant from South or Southeast Asia

migrant person who moves away from their usual place of residence to another

migration the movement of a person or people from one country or place of residence to settle in another

navvies people who are employed to do hard physical work, usually building roads, railways or canals

peddling going door to door to sell goods

persecution the unfair or cruel treatment of someone (or a group of people) over a long period of time because of their race, religion, political beliefs, sexual preferences or disability

pogrom an act of organised cruel behaviour or killing against a group of people for racial or religious reasons

prejudice an unreasonable dislike of a particular group of people, or a preference for one group of people over another

prostitution where a person has sex in return for money

racism prejudice towards people from a particular ethnic group, typically a minority ethnic group

refugee someone forced to leave their home to escape war, persecution or a natural disaster

scapegoat a person who is blamed for wrongdoings or mistakes

sweatshop a place where people work for long hours and for very low pay in unhealthy, crowded conditions

synagogue place of worship for Jewish people

trade-unionist someone who is a member of an organisation (trade union) that tries to protect workers' rights and improve pay and conditions

Index

A
activism 56–7, 61
African-Caribbean people 13, 31, 44–59
   activism and achievement 56–7
   discrimination against 48, 50
   employment 48, 50–1
   service in armed forces 48, 57
   tensions between migrants and existing populations 50
   violence against 50, 54, 55
   'Windrush generation' 46–9
   see also Black Africans
'Africanisation' policy 72
agriculture 14, 32, 33
Albanian Kosovan refugees 78, 79
Aliens Act (1905) 21, 27
Anderson, Viv 57
Anglo-Saxons 16, 17
anti-racist groups 71
antisemitism 19, 22, 23, 25, 62
armed forces 32, 48, 57, 80–1
arts 60, 62, 75
asylum seekers 9, 78, 79
   see also refugees
atrocities 78
ayahs 30, 66

B
Bangladesh 68
Bank of England 29
Barnardo, Thomas 35
Battle of Cable Street 22–3
Beaker people 15
Beatles 37
Beharry, Johnson 57
Birmingham 36
Black Africans
   enslaved Africans 41, 43, 44, 45
   pre-20th-century presence in Britain 40–3
   see also African-Caribbean people
Blackman, Malorie 57
Blanke, John 42
'blood libel' 19
Bosniak refugees 78, 79
boycotts 50–1
Brexit 86–7
Brighton 13
Bristol Bus Boycott 50–1
'Britain', use of term 7
'Britannia' 16
British Army Auxiliary Corps 80, 81
British Brothers' League 21
British Empire 47, 66, 72, 84
British Isles 7, 17
British Union of Fascists (BUF) 22, 23
Britons 16
Bronze Age 15
business people 75

C
Cable Street, Battle of 22–3
Cameron, David 91
Caribbean 44, 46
   see also African-Caribbean people
Catholic Church 19
Celts 16
Chain, Ernst 25
Chinese migrants 29
citizenship test 79
Civil Rights movements 50
Cochrane, Kelso 55
Cohen, Jack 21
colonies 10, 12, 44
   see also empire
'colour bar' 50–1
'colour problem' 47
Commonwealth 12, 47
cricket 67, 75
crime 35, 62
Crimean War 45, 63
Cuffay, William 45
Czech migrants 80, 81

D
debt slavery 11
Desai, Jayaben 71
Dickens, Charles 62
discrimination
   against African-Caribbean people 48, 50
   against Irish people 48
   against Jewish people 19, 22, 23, 25, 62
   against South Asian people 50, 70–1, 75
   government responses to 52, 53
   see also racism
disease 35, 63
divisive issue, migration as 90

E
East African Asians 72–3
Eastern European migrants 31, 80–9
   in Britain today 86–7
   decline in migration to Britain 86–7
   employment 85, 87
   and the EU 84–5
   impact on Britain 85, 87
   service in armed forces 80–1
economic migrants 8, 86
Edward I 19, 20
emigrants 9, 53
empire 47, 66, 72, 84
Empire Road (TV series) 64
Empire Windrush 13, 44, 46, 47, 59
   see also Windrush...
employment
   African-Caribbean people 48, 50–1
   'colour bar' 50–1
   Eastern European people 85, 87
   indenture system 72
   and migration 90
   seasonal workers 87
   South Asian people 61, 66, 68–9, 70
enslaved Africans 41, 43, 44, 45
entrepreneurs 75
'European citizenship' 84
European Union (EU)
   and Brexit 86–7
   and Eastern European migration 84–5
European Voluntary Workers (EVW) scheme 82
exploitation 11

F
famine, Irish 32–3, 36
farming 14, 32, 33
films 64, 75
fines 19
First World War 45, 48
Flemish migrants 28
food culture 29, 31, 60, 75
football 45, 55, 57
forced labour 11
forced migration 8
Friendly Societies 28

G
genocide 78
Germany 22, 24, 29, 79
government
   anti-discrimination laws 52, 53
   and refugee crisis 79
Great Britain 32
'Great Hunger' 32–3, 36
Grunwick Dispute 71

H
Hackett, Roy 51
Hamilton, Sir Lewis 57
Harewood, David 64
'hate crimes' 75
Henry III 19
Henry VIII 42
Holocaust 24
Huguenots 28, 90
hunter-gatherers 14

I
immigrants 9, 53
   hostility towards 21
   illegal immigrants 93
   impact on Britain 91
Immigration Act (1971) 53
indenture system 72
India 68, 69
'Indian' restaurants 75
institutional racism 54
internment 23
Iraqi refugees 78
Irish people 30, 32–7
   blame for crime and disease 62, 63
   discrimination against 48
   famine 32–3, 36
Iron Age 15
Italian migrants 30
'Ivory Bangle Lady' 40

J
Jewish Board of Guardians 21

Migration Nation 95

Jewish people 18–21
   blame for disease 63
   'blood libel' 19
   British Jews 20–1, 25
   discrimination against 19, 22, 23, 25, 62
   in medieval England 18–19
   migration of 18, 24
   persecution of 18, 19, 24
   refugees 22, 24, 80
Jones, Claudia 56

K
Kenya 31, 72
Kindertransport 24, 80

L
lascars 30, 66
Lawrence, Stephen 54
Leicester 72–3
Lincoln 18, 19
Liverpool
   Irish communities 32, 33, 37
   Royal Albert Dock 30, 35
London
   Battle of Cable Street 22–3
   Jewish communities 20, 21, 25
   Petticoat Lane 29
   Polish communities 31, 80
   in Tudor times 41
   Whitechapel 20
Love Thy Neighbour (TV series) 64

M
Maastricht Treaty 84
Macpherson report 54
Mahomed, Sake Dean 13, 67
Manchester 32
Marks, Michael 21, 80
marriage, forced 11
media 62–5, 75, 93
Mercury, Freddie 75
migrants 6, 8, 9
   exploitation of 11
   media portrayal of 62–5
   recent arrivals in Britain 78–9
   types of 10, 28–31
   undocumented migrants 93
migration
   benefits and costs of 90, 91
   and Brexit 86–7
   controversial aspects of 90–3
   definition and terminology 9

and employment 90
facts and figures 92
forced migration 8
hidden stories 13
impact on Britain 60–1, 93
inclusive story of 13
net migration 92
opposition to 50, 52
reasons to study 6, 12–13
reports on 93
statistics of 92
voluntary migration 8
why people migrate 8, 10, 28–31, 68–9
Mile End Pogrom 23
moneylending 18
Mosley, Oswald 22, 23
mosques 61
'mother country' 12
music 60, 75

N
National Front 52, 70–1
National Health Service (NHS) 37, 47, 49, 61, 74
national identity, British 90
navvies 34, 35
Nazi Germany 22, 24, 29
net migration 92
newspapers 65, 75, 93
NHS *see* National Health Service
Normans 17
Northern Ireland 36
Notting Hill Carnival 56
nurses 37, 48, 49, 63, 74

P
Pakistan 68
Parliament 20
peddling 20
persecution 8, 18, 19, 24
   see also discrimination; racism
Picts 16
pirates 41
pogroms 20, 80
police 54
Polish migrants/refugees 31, 49, 82, 83, 87
   in 1600s and 1700s 80
   impacts of migration on Britain and Poland 85
   return to Poland 86
   service in armed forces 81
Polish Resettlement Act (1947) 81
political cartoons 27, 33, 63
'potato blight' 32
Powell, Enoch 52, 53

prejudice 54–5, 62
   see also discrimination; racism
Prince, Mary 45
prostitution 11

R
Race Relations Acts 52, 53
racism
   against African-Caribbean people 48, 50–1, 54, 55
   against Jewish people 19, 22, 23, 25, 62
   against South Asian people 50, 70–1, 75
   in the police 54
   see also discrimination
railways 34, 35, 72
Ranjitsinhji, Kumar Shri 67
refugees 8, 9, 21
   Albanian Kosovan 78, 79
   government policy 79
   Huguenot 28
   Iraqi 78
   Irish 33
   Jewish 22, 24, 80
   Polish 49
   Somalian 78
   Syrian 8, 65, 78
   Ukrainian 9, 78
religious worship 61
reports on migration 93
resettlement camps 82, 83
Romans 16, 40
Rosen, Michael 25
Royal Air Force 81

S
sailors 29, 30, 41, 66
St Patrick's Day 37
scapegoats 35
Scotland 15, 16, 30
Seacole, Mary 45, 63
seasonal workers 87
Second World War 24, 31, 69, 80–1
'settled status' 86, 87
silk-weavers 28
Singh, Sophia Duleep 67
Skara Brae, Orkney 15
'slave trade' 43, 44
slavery, modern 11
Slovak migrants 80
Somalian refugees 78
Sorabji, Cornelia 67
South Asian people 66–75
   'Asian' term 68
   British Asians 71, 74–5
   discrimination against 50, 70–1, 75

in East Africa 72–3
employment 61, 66, 68–9, 70
'hate crimes' against 75
life in Britain 70
migration of 13, 30, 31, 68–9
political activity 74
religion 74
violence against 71
statistics, use of 92
Stephenson, Paul 51
Stone Age 14, 15
strikes 71
Sunak, Rishi 74
sweatshops 21
synagogues 20, 25, 61
Syrian refugees 8, 65, 78

T
television 64
temples 61
Thakrar family 75
trade-unionists 22
transport 34, 35, 61, 72
Tudor era, Black people's presence in England 41–3
Tull, Walter 45
Türkiye (Turkey) 8

U
Uganda 31, 72, 73
Ukrainian refugees 9, 78, 79, 87
undocumented migrants 93
United Kingdom 15, 32
USA, Irish migrants in 33, 36, 37

V
Vietnamese migrants/refugees 11, 78
Vikings 17
voluntary migration 8

W
Walloon migrants 28
William the Conqueror 18
'Windrush generation' 46–9
'Windrush Scandal' 55

Y
York 19